DNA PIONEER

DNA PIONEER

James Watson and the Double Helix

Joyce Baldwin

Walker and Company
New York

First published in the United States of America in 1994 by Walker
Publishing Company, Inc.

Published simultaneously in Canada by Thomas Allen & Son
Canada, Limited, Markham, Ontario

Library of Congress Cataloging-in-Publication Data
Baldwin, Joyce.
DNA pioneer : James Watson and the double helix / Joyce Baldwin.
p.   cm.
Includes bibliographical references and index.
ISBN 0-8027-8297-3 (cloth) —ISBN 0-8027-8298-1 (lib. bdg.)
1. Watson, James D., 1928—Juvenile literature.   2. DNA—
Research—History—Juvenile literature.   3. Molecular
biologists—United States—Biography—Juvenile
literature. [1. Watson, James D., 1928- .   2. Molecular
biologists.   3. DNA—Research—History.]   I. Title.
QP620.W38B35   1994
574.87'3282'092—dc20
[B]   93-31090
CIP
AC

Printed in the United States of America

2   4   6   8   10   9   7   5   3   1

Contents

Acknowledgments

It is a pleasure to acknowledge and thank the following individuals for their valuable assistance. I am especially grateful to James D. Watson, who met with me several times and shared family photographs from his personal collection, and to his wife, Elizabeth Watson, and his sister, Elizabeth Myers. Without the talents, energy, and cooperative spirit of Susan Cooper, director of public affairs and libraries, Cold Spring Harbor Laboratory, this book would not have become a reality. Clare Bunce, archives assistant, provided marvelous assistance, always with a note of cheer. Lisa Gentry, former public affairs assistant, and Lynn Kasso, administrative secretary to the director of public affairs, were also helpful. Nathaniel C. Comfort, science writer, provided assistance on several occasions. Ms. Cooper, Mr. Comfort, and Jan A. Witkowski, Ph.D., director of Banbury Center, read the manuscript for technical accuracy. Mrs. Myers read a section of the manuscript. Their keen eyes improved the copy; I am grateful to them.

Scientists from Cold Spring Harbor Laboratory who

shared information with me include Bruce Stillman, Ph.D., assistant director, and Daniel Marshak, Ph.D., senior staff investigator. Dr. Alfred Hershey, who retired as director of the genetic research unit, provided a written answer to my request, and Harriet D. ("Jill") Hershey, his wife, invited me to their home for an interview. Colleagues of James Watson's from other institutions who agreed to be interviewed are F. H. C. Crick, Ph.D., the Salk Institute; Paul Doty, Ph.D., professor emeritus of biochemistry and public policy and director emeritus of science and international affairs; Walter Gilbert, Ph.D., Carl M. Loeb university professor; Mark Ptashne, Ph.D., professor of biochemistry and molecular biology, Department of Biochemistry and Molecular Biology, all of Harvard University; Nancy Hopkins, Ph.D., professor of biology, and Phillip Sharp, Ph.D., head of the department of biology, both of the Massachusetts Institute of Technology; Joan A. Steitz, Ph.D., Henry Ford II professor of molecular biophysics and biochemistry and investigator at the Howard Hughes Medical Institute at Yale School of Medicine; Mario Capecchi, Ph.D., professor in the department of human genetics at University of Utah School of Medicine and investigator at the Howard Hughes Medical Institute; Elke Jordan, Ph.D., National Institutes of Health, National Center for Human Genome Research; Nancy S. Wexler, Ph.D., chair, joint working group on ethical, legal, and social issues, the U.S. Human Genome Working Project; Norman Kurland, Ph.D., special assistant to the president, University at Albany; William H. Grover, partner and president, Centerbrook Architects and Planners.

Margaret Hanan and Janet Unwin supplied photographs

taken especially for this book. Anne Sayre entrusted me with a rare photograph of Rosalind Franklin. I also acknowledge the help of Kristina Fallenius, information department, the Nobel Foundation; Elizabeth Sage, archives assistant, the University of Chicago Library; and Raymond Ward, New Regal Theater Foundation.

I thank Caryl Ackerman, director of the Oceanside Library in Oceanside, New York; Evelyn Rothschild, assistant director of the same institution; and their staff. I also thank Laura Frary, librarian for young adult books at the Garden City Public Library in New York. For special assistance I thank Esther Ratner, former librarian at Roslyn High School in Roslyn, New York.

I thank everyone at Walker and Company, especially Emily Easton, editorial director, books for young readers; Jeanne Gardner, field editor; Victoria Haire, copy editor; and Mary Rich, editor.

I also thank the following individuals: Joan Gaetjen Andrews; Joan Greenfield; Stewart Kampel, editor of the Long Island section of *The New York Times*; Carol Cruess Pflumm; Madeline Richardson; Jennifer Spector; Marianne Taras Sudak; and Graziella Weber-Grassi. Harriet Tremper launched me on my writing career; I wish she were here today to enjoy this project. Millicent and Brie are fascinated by the entire word-processing/fax operation, and I am fascinated by their feline antics. We are more than compatible office companions.

Jim Baldwin, my husband, adds great love, grace, intelligence, and sensitivity to my life. His focus on my work enriches the product and my enjoyment of the process. As the Latin phrase sine qua non so eloquently expresses—without him, nothing.

Author's Note

Several years ago I, like millions of other Americans, read *The Double Helix* and met in its pages the brash, young Dr. James Watson, who at age twenty-five had made one of the foremost scientific discoveries of this century. His book provided an intriguing look at science, told from his special vantage point. As a biology teacher at Roslyn High School on Long Island, New York, I taught teenagers the rudimentary characteristics of DNA and pointed out that Watson was director of Cold Spring Harbor Laboratory, only a few miles away.

In 1988, as a stringer for the *New York Times* Long Island Section, I landed an assignment to do a question-and-answer piece on Watson, and he granted my request for an interview. He had recently been appointed to head the National Center for Human Genome Research and was juggling the demands of that position and his responsibilities as director of the laboratory. His time was so tightly scheduled that it was six weeks before an appointment could be arranged. We met for nearly two hours in Watson's comfortable, orderly office affording views of the harbor. He spoke of his work, his plans for the laboratory and the genome project, and of the time almost forty years earlier when he and Dr. Francis Crick had made their landmark discovery of the double helix. He proudly showed me his Nobel Prize award, hanging then in an alcove of his office. Before I left, he presented me with a copy of the Norton Critical Edition of *The Double Helix* and inscribed the book. The inspiration for this book grew out of that interview.

In the autumn of 1991, I wrote to Susan Cooper, director of public affairs and libraries of Cold Spring Harbor Laboratory, outlining my proposal to write a biography about James Watson for young adults. Within a week, Watson agreed to be interviewed for this project. From January to September 1992, we met four times in his office at the laboratory. On one occasion I met his wife, Elizabeth Watson, at Blackford Hall for lunch and an extensive walk on the laboratory grounds. As we made our way down Bungtown Road, the narrow blacktop road where so many distinguished scientists have walked during the last century, we stopped at the frog pond and spoke with Dr. Barbara McClintock, who won a Nobel Prize for her findings on "jumping genes."

Elizabeth Myers, Watson's sister, welcomed me to her Manhattan penthouse for an interview about their childhood. Francis Crick spoke with me from La Jolla; it was a lively conversation punctuated by bits of humor. Colleagues of Watson's from Cold Spring Harbor Laboratory and other laboratories were gracious in their willingness to be interviewed either in person or by telephone.

I spent many hours researching print and photographic materials in the laboratory's Archives, tucked under the roof of the Carnegie Library. Susan Cooper also made available armloads of videotapes, which were valuable additions to the other research materials. All dialogue in *DNA Pioneer, James Watson and the Double Helix* is directly quoted from personal interviews, direct correspondence, published interviews, or videotapes.

DNA PIONEER

Introduction: Spectacular Possibilities

The ring of the telephone broke the early-morning quiet in James Watson's Cambridge, Massachusetts, home on October 18, 1962. Who could be calling so early? He was getting ready to go to Harvard University, where he headed the laboratory of molecular biology. What could be so urgent that the caller was ringing at this hour? He lifted the receiver and listened to the speaker on the other end of the wire. This was no ordinary telephone call. The call was from Sweden, which explained the early hour since European time is six hours ahead of that of the eastern United States. In Sweden the workday already was well under way. A reporter at a Swedish radio station was calling to announce that Watson had won a Nobel Prize in the category "physiology or medicine" for his discovery of the structure of deoxyribonucleic acid (DNA). He shared the prize and $50,000 with Drs. Francis Crick and Maurice Wilkins.

The award, the most prestigious of all science honors, was created by Alfred Nobel, the inventor of dynamite. In a will of less than 300 words he stipulated in November of 1895 that most of his $9 million estate should be invested to fund prizes "to those who during the preceding year have conferred the greatest benefit on mankind." In addition to the physiology or medicine category, Nobel listed physics, chemistry, literature, and peace (which he called "fraternity among nations"). The first awards were presented in 1901.

"I was very pleased, but I can't say I was totally surprised," said Watson. "People had been telling me, 'You're going to get it,' but my father was more certain than I." Indeed, many people had been predicting for years that one day he would be awarded the Nobel Prize for the discovery of DNA, one of the most significant scientific breakthroughs of the twentieth century. In 1960 Watson, Crick, and Wilkins had been honored by an award presented by the Albert and Mary Lasker Foundation, often an indication that a Nobel Prize would soon follow.

Word of the Nobel award spread rapidly over news wires and radio and television broadcasts. As Watson's colleagues drove to work, they heard the announcement on their car radios and rushed to congratulate him. Students in his class wrote in big block letters on the blackboard: "Dr. Watson has just won the Nobel Prize!" Classes were informal as the day became one of celebration with champagne toasts. "The whole day was essentially wasted," said one of the scientists working in Watson's Harvard laboratory, adding, "but joyfully." A photographer snapped a picture as Watson addressed his class. It appeared in *The New York Times* the next day with a front-page article announcing the news. A headline in *Time* magazine labeled the three winners "Nucleic Noblemen."

James Watson, who has a dry sense of humor, did not let the occasion escape without a wry comment. "It is an important thing we have accomplished," he told a reporter, "but we have not done away with the common cold—which I now have." It was indeed an important accomplishment. One measure of the significance of the discovery was that many other Nobel Prizes awarded during the second half of the twentieth century stemmed from it. By determining the DNA structure, Watson, Crick, and Wilkins had learned the "secret of life"—how genetic information is passed from one generation to another. Discovering the DNA double helix was a brilliant achievement.

The Nobel Prize was officially presented at a ceremony in Stockholm on December 10, 1962, the sixty-sixth anniversary of Nobel's death. Watson, his father, and his sister, Betty, flew to Sweden for the award ceremony. They stayed at the Old Grand Hotel in Stockholm and enjoyed several days of celebration in the snowy city. The presentation ceremony was majestic. The men wore tuxedos, and the women wore elegant ball gowns and elbow-length white kid gloves. James Watson was handsome in white tie and tails, his hair slicked into place. He and his colaureates listened attentively as the presentations were made by the king of Sweden, Gustaf VI, in the grand ballroom. "The formulation of the double helical structure of the deoxyribose nucleic acid with the specific pairing of the organic bases opens the most spectacular

*Dr. James D. Watson smiles as he receives the 1963 Nobel Prize
in Physiology or Medicine for his role in the discovery of
DNA.   (Courtesy of Svenskt Pressfoto)*

possibilities for the unraveling of the details of the control and transfer of genetic information. It is my humble
duty to convey to you the warm congratulations of the
Royal Karolinksa Institute and to ask you to receive this
year's Nobel Prize in Physiology or Medicine from the
hands of His Majesty the King," said Dr. A. V. Engs-
trom, a professor of the institute. Watson moistened his
lips, betraying a slight nervousness, and watched as Crick
walked the few steps to receive his award. There was a
trumpet fanfare and applause. Then it was his turn. He

walked steadily toward the king. "I have great pleasure in handing you this award; my very best wishes for continued excellent work in your science," said the king of Sweden. The two men shook hands. "Thank you," said Watson.

Clasped in his left hand were a gold medal with a likeness of Alfred Nobel and a handsome certificate inscribed in Swedish and decorated with a specially commissioned artwork. He was only thirty-four years old, one of the youngest men to be honored by the Nobel Foundation. A trumpet fanfare and applause sounded once again as Watson bowed.

Assembled guests applaud Watson, who has just accepted the Nobel Prize.   (Courtesy of Pressens Bild)

1

Blue-winged Warblers

The hoopla of the Roaring Twenties, with its speak-easies, bootleg booze, and the Charleston, was on the verge of giving way to the Great Depression of the 1930s when James Dewey Watson was born April 6, 1928. His parents, James Dewey and Margaret Jean Watson, were understandably proud of their firstborn child. The middle name that Jimmy and his father shared was the family name of several prominent Americans, including John Dewey, the educator, and Thomas Dewey, the politician. These Deweys and members of both sides of Jimmy's family traced their roots to ancestors who had emigrated from England and arrived in Boston in 1630.

Two years after the birth of Jimmy, his sister, Elizabeth, was born in June 1930. The four Watsons lived in a neighborhood on the south side of Chicago, at first in a rented apartment and then in a house in a neighbor-hood between the steel mills and the University of Chicago. Their bungalow was a low brick building with a peaked roof, under which was an atticlike area that provided bedrooms for Jimmy and Betty. On warm summer nights the family gathered on their small front porch to visit with neighbors. The block was home to many children of both Irish and Jewish backgrounds, a community-oriented group where everyone knew one another. There was an apartment building next door to the Watsons and a hospital down the street. Some of the houses on the block were older than theirs and some newer, but many were small bungalows, just like theirs.

Jimmy lived a life much like that of all the other kids on the block, but his passion for getting at the truth set him apart from the others. His curiosity caught people's attention. He always asked, "Why, why, why?" He didn't tolerate simplistic answers and persisted with questions until he was satisfied. He wanted to know how the world worked.

Jimmy attended the University of Chicago Nursery School and then Horace Mann Elementary School, walking to school with his sister and coming home for lunch. Everybody knew he was a bright young boy. He learned quickly and was fond of reading and remembering the vast array of facts in the *World Almanac*. Not every subject appealed to him, though he took a great interest in learning about the ones that caught his attention. The others he ignored. "Fortunately, no one tried to make me well rounded," he later said, adding that he thought it important for teachers to "focus more on our unique features and encourage them."

Jimmy was curious about his IQ. "So when my grammar school teacher wasn't around, I looked up my IQ and it was pretty low, that is, around 120," he once told a journalist. His IQ score was not low by general standards, but Jimmy thought it was low because he was comparing it to genius level. His teachers knew that one isolated test does not necessarily assess a child's ability. They also knew that Jimmy was highly intelligent. His questions always probed beyond the lesson at hand. Sometimes they stumped his teachers. "I have to go home at night and study to be one step ahead of little Jimmy Watson," a teacher told his mother, "because he's always one step ahead of me." He skipped two half grades in grammar school, and his peers quickly singled him out as being "smart." The grading system of the Chicago public schools rated students' work as fair, good, excellent, and superior, a scale that taught Jimmy that he had to be better than excellent to be on top.

Jimmy had friends, but he was shy. And friends were not the most important part of his life. He had no interest in many of his grammar school classmates, in part because politics was important to him and they didn't share his views. When he was only eight years old, Jimmy followed the 1936 presidential election closely. Most of his classmates sported sunflower pins to advertise their support for Alf Landon, the Republican candidate. Jimmy and his family backed Franklin Roosevelt, a Democrat, who was reelected to the presidency that year, and later for two more terms. His mother was a precinct captain active in local politics. She worked to get the vote out, going door-to-door encouraging people to cast their votes.

The Watson children were special in another way that was noticed by their classmates. Jimmy and Betty had permission to leave school early one Wednesday a month, an opportunity their classmates envied. They attended concerts for youngsters presented by the Chicago Symphony Orchestra, which was conducted by Frederick Stock. Both Betty and Jimmy enjoyed the concerts and also liked to listen to classical music on the radio at home.

Jimmy Watson also distinguished himself from his schoolmates when he appeared on the "Quiz Kids," a popular radio program. He was the winner on several shows and garnered a $100 war bond as a prize, even though the questions weren't directed toward his interest in subjects such as world affairs. Eventually he lost to a girl steeped in Bible stories. His version of why he lost was that she knew more than he did about the Old Testament. Betty thought he just wasn't the brightest or most scintillating contestant and that the producers didn't think he had enough audience appeal.

Jimmy and Betty enjoyed playing together, finding pleasure in simple, inexpensive activities. Their family, like many others caught in the Depression, managed with little money. The Watson children loved to roller-skate up and down the block and ride their bicycles after school; in the fall they liked to help with raking and burning leaves, a ritual that provided the neighbors with an informal chance to socialize while doing a pleasant chore. "It was a very normal childhood," his sister later recalled. Jimmy and Betty enjoyed playing Boot the Can and Hide and Seek with neighborhood pals. During three summers beginning when Jimmy was about ten, he

*Jimmy Watson at about ten years of age with his father and his
sister, Betty.   (Courtesy of Cold Spring Harbor Laboratory Archives)*

and his sister spent a month at a "host" farm in Allegan,
Michigan. While there, the children went swimming in
a lake, collected freshly laid eggs, and watched the farm-
ers do their threshing.

Betty took piano lessons; Jimmy wasn't as keen about
playing, but he liked to join his sister in duets. "He
wasn't very good," his sister said. "I was much better."
But the children never argued about who was a better
piano player or, for that matter, about anything else.

Saturday afternoons they often went to the movies
with their friends, walking to the Avalon Theater on
Seventy-ninth and Stony Island Avenue and paying
twenty-five cents admission to see the latest Hollywood

Jimmy and Betty play a duet at the piano in 1940. (Courtesy of Cold Spring Harbor Laboratory Archives)

film. It was always a great event; the youngsters enjoyed the freedom and excitement of being on their own for a day. The Avalon, built in 1927, was an oversized theater that accommodated more than 2,300 people. Jimmy and Betty thought they were stepping into another world when they entered the lobby, which was decorated with scenes from North Africa and the Middle East. Its designer was John Eberson, an architect who had studied in Vienna. According to one story, the architect's imagination was sparked by a Persian incense burner that he found while browsing in a New Orleans antique store. The Avalon lobby resembled a sultan's palace with exotic dancers, fountains, and ivy vines climbing palace walls and archways. Wood murals, painted with scenes of Persian royal gardens, competed for attention amid the North African influences. A ceiling mosaic that movie patrons called "The Flying Carpet" was a plaster version of an Oriental carpet, encrusted with jewels and cut-glass sparkles. When they went into the auditorium, the children were enchanted with the hundreds of twinkling electric lights, which gave the impression of a summer evening in a sultan's backyard.

Jimmy, Betty, and their friends nibbled their five-cent candy and watched the on-screen action from the huge balcony in the opulent, old-time theater. Vivien Leigh and Clark Gable captured their attention in *Gone with the Wind*, which won the 1939 Oscar for best picture. They also enjoyed *How Green Was My Valley*, the 1941 Oscar winner, and other classics such as *Kitty Foyle* and *Goodbye, Mr. Chips*. These films showed them worlds beyond their own. One of the films that Jimmy saw again and again was *Pygmalion*, the charming precursor to *My Fair Lady*. "I went to the movies all the time," he later explained, "because they showed you something outside the south side of Chicago." Slapstick comedy also appealed to Jimmy. He laughed heartily at the antics of the Three Stooges. That kind of bumptious humor did not appeal to Betty. While Jimmy roared at the comedy routines of Curly, Moe, and Larry, Betty sat quietly, thinking "This is really dull."

Jimmy and Betty enjoyed their parents' company and liked hearing about their family history. Margaret Jean Watson, their beautiful black-haired mother, was the only child of Elizabeth Gleason and Lauchlin Mitchell. Her father had been born in Scotland; her mother, in Ireland. Her father was orphaned at an early age and moved from Glasgow to Toronto, where he lived with an uncle. Elizabeth Gleason's family had emigrated to the

*Margaret Jean Watson,
Jimmy's mother, in a
photograph taken
about 1917.* (Courtesy
of Cold Spring Harbor
Laboratory Archives)

United States from Dublin and settled on a farm in Michigan City, Indiana, at the tip of Lake Michigan. These circuitous paths conspired to bring the couple to Chicago, where they met and married, thousands of miles from their ancestral homes. Heartbreak came early to Margaret Jean, however, when her father died of injuries suffered in an accident that happened when horses pulling a cab rampaged out of control. The accident occurred on Christmas Eve 1903, Margaret Jean's fourth birthday.

Mr. Watson's family included many accomplished people. His grandmother was a professional concert pianist, and one of his brothers, William W. Watson, was a professor and head of the physics department at Yale University. His uncle, Dudley Crafts Watson, was an artist who taught and lectured at the Art Institute of Chicago. Uncle Dudley helped raise Orson Welles, the actor and movie director and the author of "Invasion from Mars."

Jimmy's mother, who was Irish Catholic, worked during World War II as a director of personnel for the Chicago Red Cross and later in the admissions office of the University of Chicago. A gregarious woman, she liked to draw in charcoal or pen and was active in community work as president of the local Parent-Teachers Association, leader of the Brownie troop, and den mother of a pack of Cub Scouts. She loved to act and performed in a few plays produced by community theater groups.

Jimmy's father worked in the financial office of a business school and was responsible for collecting its bills. The job was not one he enjoyed, but illness had frustrated his desire to pursue a different career. Jimmy always thought his father would have been a marvelous teacher. Mr. Watson had a hobby that brought him great pleasure. He was an avid birder, almost a professional ornithologist, who had begun bird watching as a teenager. When he married, he gave up the hobby until Jimmy was old enough to go with him. For his eighth birthday, Jimmy was given a book on birds. It was his first science book and he loved it. Jimmy embraced the hobby of birding wholeheartedly, not with a childlike interest but as an adult with an intense desire to learn all about the subject. He cashed in the bond he had won on the "Quiz Kids" to buy a pair of binoculars. Father and son spent hours together searching out blue-winged warblers, scarlet tanagers, blue jays, and other birds in the parks near their home. They studied bird songs, nests, and migration habits and monitored spring migration patterns. They prowled garbage dumps, popular feeding grounds for birds, in search of species to add to their list. Jimmy's interest in birding was as passionate as his father's and served as a catalyst to pique his scientific curiosity. "It was the way I got into science," he later explained.

The Watson family had lively dinners, with the family sitting around the dining room table discussing world affairs. The elder Watsons were aware of the coming of World War II, and their radio was always tuned to a station that would inform them of recent developments. Jimmy was as interested in current events as his parents and never missed hearing a speech by President Roosevelt or Winston Churchill, the prime minister of Great Britain. Both men were great orators, and Jimmy loved to listen to them, not just for what they said but also for how they said it. "They both respected intelligence," he said. "You could just see it in their use of words." Like the movies, the radio showed Jimmy a world beyond his own. Both were strong influences on him.

The Watson library was filled with thousands of books; Jimmy's father read the reviews of new books and, to the extent he could afford it, bought the most highly recommended ones. He carefully cut out reviews from newspapers, neatly folded each one, and placed it between the covers of the relevant book. Evenings the family gathered in the living room, reading and listening to music. Jimmy loved reading. "Dad's books told me more about America than I would learn from my daily life," he once said. Jimmy and his father also made weekly trips to the library. The family did not own a car, so after supper on Friday nights, he and his father walked the mile to the public library on Seventy-third Street. There they browsed through the shelves of books, selecting their reading for the next week.

One book that set his mind whirling was *Arrowsmith*,

the novel by Sinclair Lewis about Martin Arrowsmith, a physician who becomes a laboratory researcher to search for a cure to the bubonic plague. For a long time after reading it, Jimmy thought about how exciting it would be to make great scientific discoveries.

Jimmy's interests—reading, birding, music—were those of a mature person. Not many youngsters shared his fascination with those pastimes. "Crucial to my future success were older people who appreciated me, unlike my peers whom I had no knack for putting at ease," he once said. His teachers understood him; they recommended that he leave high school after his sophomore year and helped him get a scholarship to the University of Chicago. He had vague aspirations of studying science but had not studied chemistry or physics in high school. And there was one other thing on Jimmy's mind. "With my low IQ, I had to wonder whether, well, could I make it?"

2

A Growth Spurt

*J*im Watson was only fifteen years old and five feet, three inches tall when he entered the University of Chicago as a freshman in a program for gifted youngsters. He spent a few days in the summer orientation session in a small house next to the college chapel; the private residence had been converted into a dormitory and had rooms of varying sizes. After that brief introduction to dorm life, Norman Kurland, who had shared a room with Jim for a few days, continued to live on campus, but Jim lived at home. He was a skinny, awkward adolescent—very intense, very bright, and very pleasant, but with little ambition to gain friends. He wasn't a typical teenager. "I never even tried to be an adolescent," he said. "I never went to teenage parties. I never tried to talk like a teenager. That probably made people dislike me. . . . I didn't fit in. I didn't want to fit in. I basically passed from being a child to an adult."

Chancellor Robert Hutchins had initiated a program called the Great Books, so named because the curriculum was based on the reading of classics. Bright students were admitted to college after only two years of high school. The 1945–46 school catalog described Hutchins's innovative approach. It stated that "the requirements for the Bachelor's degree at Chicago are met by passing comprehensive examinations—rather than by earning credit in individual courses."

In courses that Jim liked, biology and social sciences, he earned A's; but in math he drew a B and in English, a C. It was at Chicago that he began to judge his capabilities. "You won't find out how good you are unless you go to a place that's tops, and then you find yourself in a certain level," he said. "I discovered I was never going to be a philosopher." But zoology—which "I knew I could do"—began to take on more importance. He was beginning to understand the direction his life would take. He found that "Hutchins had scorn for the trivial" and that emphasis on ideas rather than memorization of dates and facts enabled students to learn how to "draw a big picture" and "see what moves civilization, why things really happened." Jim also found it valuable that "Chicago was an extremely critical place."

Later Jim would offer advice to students making a decision about where to study. "Go to a college where, when you get there, you think your peers are brighter than you are," he said. "Try to go to a place where you will be challenged. Otherwise you never really know how good you are."

Jim seldom took notes in class, a trait that some of his teachers found insulting. But, to Jim, taking notes and absorbing what the professor was saying were incompatible. "If you take notes, you can't think," he said. Still, his zoology teacher was irritated at this habit and noticed that Jim preferred gazing out the window to watch for an attractive girl to pass. Somehow the method seemed to work for Jim: He earned an A in the course. He also earned a top grade in two botany courses. His professor later said, "He took two courses under me and received an A in both. He must have been very keen, because I don't give very many A's."

Thinking was an important activity for Jim, who enjoyed reading at a fast clip of 400 to 500 words a minute. A favorite pastime was going to the university library. "I was always excited about reading books," he said, "generally the ones I didn't understand." One day he pulled a book off the shelf that would have a lasting effect on his life. It was a newly published volume by Erwin Schrödinger. The slim ninety-six-page book, *What Is Life? The Physical Aspect of the Living Cell,* was based on lectures given at Trinity College in Dublin during February 1943. Jim's eyes lit up when he read it. This was fascinating stuff! Dr. Schrödinger's style hinted at the great secrets locked inside genes, the structures that carry the hereditary message from one generation to another. "The chromosome structures are . . . instrumental in bringing about the development they foreshadow. They are law-code and executive power—or, to use another simile, they are architect's plan and builder's craft in one."

Jim knew the "architect's plan" contained the "secret of life"—information to build an organism. He was fascinated with the idea of finding out the secret of life, of discovering how the molecules within a cell could mastermind such a feat. To unlock the secret would indeed be an accomplishment. But scientists were not even sure what kind of chemical carried the genetic information. Some thought it was a type of nucleic acid called deoxyribonucleic acid (DNA); others believed it was protein.

Jim was extremely curious about this subject. "Beginning in my junior year I dreamed I might someday work in a lab that would finally reveal the nature of life. . . . From the moment I read Schrödinger's *What Is Life?*, I became polarized toward finding out the secret of the gene," he said. But he was still a teenager, a young undergraduate student. How would he begin to solve such a complex puzzle?

Perhaps it would be better to concentrate on realistic goals. Birding was a field in which he could envision working. He would become the curator of ornithology at the Museum of Natural History. That was a sensible idea. As he looked ahead to graduating in June 1947, Jim decided to pursue graduate studies and applied to several schools. He became a bit nervous when both California Institute of Technology and Harvard University rejected his applications. Indiana University, however, accepted him and offered a $900 fellowship. A note from the dean of the graduate school was attached to the acceptance saying that he might be disappointed to find that Indiana did not offer ornithology courses and suggesting that if birding was still Jim's first interest, he should attend another school. But in his senior year, Jim—who by now had reached his full height of six feet, two inches—had decided to study genetics, and Indiana held great appeal to him.

Jim's adviser at the University of Chicago had recommended he apply to Indiana because of its strong reputation in genetics. The faculty included Nobel laureate

Dr. H. J. Muller, who had demonstrated that the rate of mutation increased when fruit flies were exposed to X rays. There were several other notable faculty members in the biology department, including Drs. Tracy M. Sonneborn, Ralph Cleland, and Salvador E. Luria.

As Jim went about his fall routine of classes as a graduate student, he wondered which research project he should pursue. Studying with H. J. Muller would be a prestigious opportunity. But as an organism for research, the fruit fly, in Jim's view, had seen "better days." The bacteriophage (also known simply as the phage), a virus that affects bacteria, caught his interest. Jim took a course with Salvador Luria, who was studying these microorganisms. The rumor among students was that Luria was "arrogant toward people who were wrong." Although there were forty students in the course, too many for teacher and student to be in close contact, Jim says he "saw no evidence of the rumored inconsiderateness toward dimwits." At the end of the term, he asked Luria if he might do his thesis project in the lab.

"He was a very remarkable fellow," Luria later said. "Even more odd then, than later. But tremendously intelligent, with this mixture of self-assurance and uncertainty of himself that very often bright kids have. . . . He is a person who looks completely disheveled all the time, a mess—except in things that matter. I have never known anybody whose notebooks, for example, were so perfect, as Jim's notebooks." Luria promptly accepted Jim and set him to work on a project related to his own research on the effect of ultraviolet light on phages. Jim's doctoral thesis was to determine how X rays affected the reproductive ability of phages.

Although Jim had arrived in Indiana wondering, "Am I going to be able to have ideas?" he soon found acceptance among the accomplished scientists. "They accepted me," he said. "I realized I could be in the same world and understand their arguments and we could disagree." He found an intellectual home in the phage group, a small informal band of scientists interested in studying the phage. Because phages consist only of a DNA core surrounded by a protein "coat," the researchers thought that by studying them they would learn more about genes. Members of the phage group worked at laboratories across the country and kept in touch with one another, getting together at meetings from time to time. Shortly after he began to work in Luria's lab, Jim met Dr. Max Delbrück, a scientist whose work had been featured in Schrödinger's book. "I easily identified with Max because he was tall and thin," he said. "He played tennis; I wanted to play tennis. His wife was very pretty, and I liked her." He was surprised by Delbrück's youthful appearance. "Though he had passed forty, Max still looked incredibly young, yet acted more than profound," he said. "Afterward he treated me like a son, and I could not see enough of him or his wife, Manny." Jim fit in easily with the bright scientists who formed the phage group. They all liked to talk science incessantly and exchange bold ideas.

In the summer the phage group gathered at Cold Spring Harbor Laboratory on Long Island Sound for meetings and to learn the latest research findings. The opportunity to spend time by the water with some of the top scientists in the world was one that Jim relished. "As the summer passed on," he said, "I liked Cold Spring

Harbor more and more, both for its intrinsic beauty and for the honest ways in which good and bad science got sorted out." Accommodations were simple summer cabins, but the country atmosphere and intense interest in science was without compare.

Jim and Renato Dulbecco, an Italian scientist working in Luria's lab, liked to relax by the harbor. They went swimming, canoeing, and clamming. In the evening Jim and other scientists played baseball or went into town for a beer at Neptune's Cave. Excitement in the quiet rural atmosphere came in the form of practical jokes. One evening Jim and several other pranksters spotted the cars of friends parked at Neptune's Cave and fiendishly deflated the tires. They were rewarded for their efforts by having their beds doused with buckets of water.

After the summer respite, Jim returned to Indiana. In 1950 he was awarded a doctorate degree in zoology. Luria arranged for him to work with Dr. Herman Kalckar in Copenhagen in the hope that Jim would learn enough biochemistry to help in studying the gene. After spending a month at Cal Tech and a few weeks at Cold Spring Harbor, young Dr. Watson sailed to Europe. The arrangement in Kalckar's lab proved disappointing, but Jim's interest in learning about the secret of life deepened. So after a year, he moved to the Cavendish Laboratory of Cambridge University in England in order to pursue that work.

3

Jolly Good Collaborators

Francis Crick heard about Jim Watson before he met him. When Watson arrived at Cambridge, another scientist introduced him to the staff members. One of the stops on the informal tour was Crick's apartment. Odile Crick later reported to her husband that a young American had come by to say hello. "And, you know what?" she told him. "He had no hair." Watson did have hair, but he had a crew cut, a style that was popular in America but considered strange in England. His hair was not his only touch of eccentricity. Watson's style of dress was casual—untidy to some eyes. He wore sneakers and went about with his shirttail untucked. "He didn't look like a person who was going to be a dean or a president of a college," said Crick. "He seemed disorganized. He got up late, went out to breakfast, played tennis in the afternoon."

Jim Watson's informal dress gave no indication of the precise manner with which he handled scientific data. *That* received his most careful attention; his notebooks were meticulously well ordered, written in his small, printlike handwriting. He used colored inks to keep track of various experiments, a system that gave him quick access to information.

He had a first-class scientific mind and a talent for selecting scientific problems to solve. Knowing what to tackle, being able to sort from all possible puzzles the one that will yield under probing, the one that will open the door to important research, is a gift of the highest order. Jim Watson was well endowed with that ability.

Watson's scientific intuition led him to believe that DNA was the hereditary material and that determining its structure would be a great discovery. While working in Kalckar's lab, Jim had attended a scientific meeting in Naples in the spring of 1951. There he heard a talk given by Dr. Maurice Wilkins from King's College in London. Wilkins was using X-ray crystallography to study DNA. The technique involves taking X-ray pictures of crystals and analyzing them mathematically in order to learn how a molecule is constructed. During his lecture, Wilkins showed an X-ray diffraction photograph of DNA. To the untrained eye it looked like a hazy, blurry X ray in shades of gray. But it snapped Watson to attention. The picture showed, as he later wrote, that "genes could crystallize; hence they must have a regular structure that could be solved in a straightforward manner."

Watson and Crick knew that the molecule governing genetics is unique. Hereditary material provides cells with information to build an organism. Genes determine whether one will have blue eyes or hazel, brown hair or blond, and they influence other traits as well, including, perhaps, personality. The arrangement of atoms in the molecule carrying the "secret of life" has to be simple enough to ensure error-free copies yet capable of endless variety to produce a wide array of traits. Many scientists thought that DNA was the molecule that carried the hereditary message from one generation to another. Others set their sights on protein as the mastermind of the genetic process. Watson and Crick threw their support to the DNA camp. They based their decision in part on experimental work done in the 1940s by Dr. Oswald T. Avery and his co-workers that pointed to DNA as the hereditary material.

It was already known that DNA consists of thousands of building blocks called nucleotides. Each nucleotide contains a sugar (deoxyribose), a phosphate group, and a nitrogen-containing base. The nitrogen-containing base can be one of four types, called A, T, C, and G in a chemical shorthand that uses the first letters of their names, which are adenine, thymine, cytosine, and guanine. The trick was to explain how these nucleotides fit together in the macromolecule of DNA.

There was a long list of unanswered questions: How did the parts link together? Were the sugar and phosphate groups on the inside of the chain? Or on the outside? How did the nitrogen-containing bases pair up? Were there three strands? Or four? Or just two? If there were two or more strands, how were they arranged?

Crick had been blocked from studying DNA because Maurice Wilkins of King's College in London had a prior claim to the research. In England, unlike the United

States, a kind of scientific politeness, coupled with funding concerns, made it awkward for Crick to study DNA. But when Watson and he met, each fired the other's enthusiasm, and they became excited by the idea of decoding the gene. Watson especially was captivated by the idea and liked to daydream about how they would announce the news of the discovery in a scientific paper.

Crick thought that he and Watson were "jolly good collaborators." The fact that neither of them had been assigned to work on DNA—Watson was "supposed" to work on myoglobin, a protein—didn't faze them. They simply fit in their discussions around the other work. "No one should mind if, by spending only a few hours a week thinking about DNA, he [Francis] helped me solve a smashingly important problem," wrote Watson in *The Double Helix*, his account of their discovery. They talked and talked and talked about how to crack the puzzle of DNA. They talked so much that their colleagues arranged for them to share a laboratory soon after Watson's arrival at the Cavendish Laboratory. The Cavendish is a modern brick building set among the ancient buildings that comprise Cambridge University, which is about fifty miles northeast of London. The room where Watson and Crick worked is about fifteen or sixteen feet long with high ceilings, a typical laboratory setting.

Francis Crick was then thirty-five years old, working toward his doctorate degree (which he received in 1954) and studying the structure of proteins using X-ray crystallography. His razor-sharp mind and his ability to spot the relevance of an experiment were envious traits. He was a genial man with a distinct laugh and the uncommon ability to cut to the heart of a matter. His tendency to interpret the meaning of other scientists' work more quickly than they did themselves, however, was a matter of concern to his colleagues, who worried he might show them up to their boss.

Crick and Watson often took a lunch break together, taking the one- or two-minute walk to the old-fashioned Eagle Pub across the road. The centuries-old Eagle had a cozy atmosphere, its ceilings decorated with messages scribbled during World War II by members of the air force. The two friends ate the standard pub fare, fish and chips, or a simple meat platter, a vegetable, and a sweet. At times, they downed a beer before taking their habitual stroll back to the laboratory by a roundabout route along the "backs," the garden and lawn area behind the university buildings that ran along the River Cam. On a pleasant day they might go punting, the term used to describe a ride in a flat-bottomed boat propelled by a long pole. While they were punting, the two scientists tossed ideas back and forth in lively conversation.

They talked, too, over dinner at the Crick apartment. "Jim would often drop around a little before dinner with a hungry look in his eye," said Crick. "We all knew what that meant—my wife was quite a good cook." The apartment was small, consisting of a living room and bedroom and a kitchen that was largely given over to a bathtub. Odile's French cooking and the chance to talk into the evening easily lured Jim Watson. It was at the Cricks' apartment that "I first sensed the vitality of English intellectual life," he later wrote, adding that he "joyously seized every opportunity to escape from the miserable English food that periodically led me to worry about whether I might have an ulcer."

Jim Watson was fervently interested in catching biology's "brass ring." He could scarcely stop thinking about it and constantly discussed the topic with Crick. But Watson did take time out for other pleasures. He enjoyed socializing, playing tennis, relaxing over a glass of sherry in the late afternoon, and dining with friends. Life for "the young scientist in a hurry" was pleasant in many ways. He wrote letters to his parents, describing his life in England. His sister, Betty was living in Denmark, and, in the summer of 1952, their mother traveled to Europe to visit with both Betty and Jim. During Mrs. Watson's three-week trip, she also traveled to Scotland and Austria with Jim. Sometime after their mother's visit, Betty moved from Denmark to Cambridge and lived there during the time her brother and Crick were most involved in DNA research. It was "such great fun, going to parties with Jim and his friends" and being "in the midst of an enormous amount of science activity which never stopped from dawn to dusk," she said. Even as a non-scientist, Betty found it exciting to see such a high level of curiosity. She, too, wrote frequent letters to her parents. "I can still see Francis and Jim walking along the river and talking nonstop," she recalled, adding how important it is in science "to have a collaborator or mentor, who can say 'No,' that's not right or 'Yes, let's explore that.'"

While in Cambridge, Betty boarded in a beautiful home at 8 Scroope Terrace owned by Camille "Pop" Prior, who rented rooms to several young Frenchwomen. The connection with Pop, who served evening meals to a few students, had been made by Jim Watson, whose stomach was at war with the English food and who wel-

*Jim Watson and his sister, Betty, in Copenhagen in the summer
of 1951.*   (Courtesy of Cold Spring Harbor Laboratory Archives)

comed the chance to dine on Pop's French cooking. Watson had an eye for the Frenchwomen, too, though he
said, "I wasn't the sort of person you asked to go to a
dinner party when I was twenty-two. I would neither
amuse them nor put them at ease. The only thing I cared
about was the gene—and girls."

DNA was a complex problem. Watson and Crick had
decided that the most fruitful approach to understanding
its structure would be to build models. "The essential
trick," Watson wrote, "was to ask which atoms like to sit
next to each other." So they set to work with a set of
building blocks—a scientific version of Tinkertoys.
Building models was an inspired idea, the mark of a certain kind of genius who understands the nature of a prob-

lem and how to go about solving it expeditiously. Dr. Linus Pauling, the great chemist who later won two Nobel Prizes, had successfully used models in his study of proteins. Watson and Crick's decision to use this approach was triggered by Pauling's success with the method. Although model building might seem simplistic, it is a highly creative way of approaching science and problem solving, and requires a sophisticated knowledge of mathematics and chemistry. Pauling was interested in DNA, too. Watson's adrenaline level increased when he thought of the possibility of beating Pauling at his own game.

There were some manic phases of his and Crick's research—times when they were so caught up in their quest that they talked about it nonstop—at dinner, at films, and late into the night. Occasionally, inspiration struck on a Saturday night, and they would get into the lab by climbing up the drainpipe and going in through a window. Some of the information took shape during quieter times such as when Watson played tennis, took walks, and admired flowers. This is often how science progresses—outside the laboratory and away from the work site. The answer to a difficult problem is not always conveniently available within a nine-to-five time frame. For scientists, there is no typical workday; life flows in and around work and, with any luck, helps it along.

A close look at a good X-ray picture of DNA might save Watson and Crick months of work. They hoped one might be available from the King's College group, but a complicated situation had developed there between Dr. Maurice Wilkins and Dr. Rosalind Franklin. Franklin, an expert X-ray crystallographer, had moved in 1950 from

Dr. Rosalind Franklin in Paris in the summer of 1948. She carries coffee served in laboratory glassware. (Courtesy of Anne Sayre)

the Laboratoire Central des Services Chimiques de l'Etat in Paris to King's College in London. The move had not proved completely satisfactory. From their first meeting, Wilkins and Franklin did not get along. Wilkins, for example, treated her as an assistant; yet she was a senior staff member, every bit his equal. For this reason and a number of others, they barely spoke, a situation not conducive to a worthwhile collaboration. Franklin was a shy woman, pleasant yet firmly professional. She never was able to establish the camaraderie with her colleagues in London that she had enjoyed in Paris, partly because of the discrimination she encountered at King's College. In Paris she had been well accepted, but she did not find King's College to be as pleasant. Although women were better accepted at King's than at some other schools, discrimination existed. The men, for example, lunched in a pleasant dining hall while the women, including the most senior staff, had the choice of either eating in the student dining room or finding a private place to have lunch. So Wilkins and Franklin had no opportunity to meet informally and perhaps smooth out their differences. Their interpersonal difficulties thwarted Watson's and Crick's hopes of quickly obtaining the X-ray data they needed.

Rosalind Franklin, however, was planning to give a seminar about her work. Watson seized the opportunity. He studied about X-ray crystallography so that he would be able to understand her talk. But at the seminar he followed his usual practice of not taking notes and came away with little information. The complexities of X-ray crystallography, a subject relatively new to him, left him with only vague remembrances of Franklin's data. Crick was disappointed with Watson's hazy report of the seminar, but on the basis of Watson's memory of the data, he determined that only a few models would fit the X-ray information. Within a few days after Franklin's talk, the two men set to work in earnest on a model of a small portion of a DNA molecule. Although Franklin had not addressed the subject of a helical structure of DNA in her lecture, Watson and Crick hoped their model building would demonstrate that DNA was in the shape of a helix. "Any other type of configuration would be much more complicated," Watson wrote, adding that worrying about complications before ruling out a simple answer would be "damned foolishness."

Watson and Crick theorized that the sugar (deoxyribose) and the phosphate group formed the backbone on the inside of the helix. The two scientists arranged and rearranged the parts of their model, trying to make them fit the data. Determining the number of strands in the helix, the type of bond that held certain atoms together, the angle of bonding, and all the chemical rules of bonding occupied their attention as they wrestled with the model. It wasn't an easy task, but after several hours' work they completed it. They were, as Watson wrote, in "ebullient spirits" as they left the lab to have dinner at the Cricks' apartment. The structure of DNA was within their grasp!

The next day they called Wilkins and invited him to Cambridge to see the model. Wilkins, Franklin, and two other scientists arrived the next morning. Watson and Crick were delighted to explain their DNA model to the small group. As the presentation got under way, however, Franklin quickly dampened their enthusiasm. She did not embrace the idea of building models as an appropriate approach, though in this case that was beside the point. Their model simply didn't fit the data she had presented at her seminar. Watson's usually excellent memory had let him down. "The awkward truth became apparent that the correct DNA model must contain at least ten times more water than was found in our model," he wrote.

Watson and Crick were crestfallen, but there was nothing to do but put the disaster behind them and enjoy the upcoming Christmas holidays. Watson spent the vacation at the Scottish country home of a friend; Betty joined him. Before Watson left Cambridge, he and Crick made an important decision about their DNA model: In order to "fit" the data, the sugar-phosphate chain had to be on the outside, not the inside of the molecule. Upon his return to Cambridge in January, Watson began to study the tobacco mosaic virus as his official research project, while continuing to be engrossed in studying DNA. He became even more interested in the concept of helical structures. "In the spring of 1952 I became very manic about the helical structure existing everywhere," said Watson. He couldn't get his mind off the helix. During a weekend visit to Oxford he spotted several spiral staircases and became increasingly convinced that both the tobacco mosaic virus and other biological structures were helixes. Indeed his research soon *confirmed* that the tobacco mosaic virus was a helical structure. With that triumph, he focused his attention squarely on DNA and added another piece of important information to his and Crick's DNA information bank: Dr. Erwin Chargaff, a biochemist, had determined that in DNA the amounts of A equal the amounts of T, and the amounts of G equal the amounts of C. How, they wondered, could these facts be used to explain the DNA structure?

As the two collaborators pursued their interest in DNA, a twist of fate brought Peter Pauling, son of Linus Pauling, to the Cavendish to work toward his doctorate degree. He shared an office with Watson and Crick and occasionally read them letters from his father that indicated his interest in solving the DNA puzzle. The idea of being in competition with Linus Pauling to discover the structure of DNA energized Jim Watson. The race was about to heat up.

4

An Elegant Molecule

*D*uring the fall of 1952 the specter of Linus Pauling solving the DNA puzzle haunted Jim Watson. A letter written in December from Pauling to his son, Peter, announced that he had determined the DNA structure. A month later another letter included the news that a manuscript had been prepared. A few weeks later Peter received a copy of it. He stuffed the manuscript into his overcoat and walked to the Cavendish. He knew it would be met with great interest. When Watson saw the paper sticking out of Peter's pocket, he could not contain his curiosity. He snatched it without waiting for Peter to hand it to him. His pulse raced as he quickly read the introduction, summary, and data.

Something seemed amiss. Was it possible that Pauling had made a mistake? Scrutinizing the figures, Watson spotted an error, an elementary chemical mistake involving the charge on the atoms. The structure Pauling had postulated would not hold together. Amazingly, he had overlooked basic chemical facts. Watson was gleeful. There was still a chance for him and Crick to win the race. "Though the odds still appeared against us, Linus had not yet won his Nobel," he wrote.

Being able to see a good X-ray crystallography picture of DNA took on extra urgency. Watson headed for London and a visit with Wilkins to show him the Pauling manuscript. While waiting to see Wilkins, he went into Franklin's laboratory. We can only guess at the subtle interplay of personalities that shifted the conversation into an unpleasant mode. Watson and "Rosy"—that was the denigrating nickname he and others called her behind her back, never to her face—began arguing about whether or not DNA was a helical structure. She was strongly opposed to the idea and became increasingly angry. Then, as Watson described the somewhat comical scene, she "came from behind the lab bench that separated us and began moving toward me. Fearing that in her hot anger she might strike me, I grabbed the Pauling manuscript and hastily retreated to the open door." At that moment Wilkins entered the lab and eased Watson's retreat. The encounter had the effect of uniting the two men in an alliance, cemented by the fact that Watson had seen firsthand the difficulties Wilkins faced in dealing with Rosalind Franklin.

Sometimes a sour situation can be turned around, but it seems that in this case neither the male scientists nor Franklin had the interpersonal skills to do so. "She thought Jim was being aggressive and abrasive," said Watson's sister. "He was just being awkward." Crick also noticed the uncomfortable relationship. "Rosalind wasn't very nice to him, although she might have had some justification," he said. "She was very impatient with Jim and wouldn't take him seriously. I think the fault was on Rosalind's side. Jim was behaving a little bit brashly, but I think she overreacted."

What were Franklin's feelings when she closed the door behind the men? It was *her* hard-earned expertise in X-ray crystallography that was yielding crucial data necessary for describing the structure of DNA. And it was wrong for Wilkins to treat her as an assistant. She was dedicated to her work; her life was devoted to science, and she was terribly disappointed at the way things were working out at King's College. The lack of professional friends was personally dispiriting and professionally wounding. Although Franklin was not a feminist, she could not help but notice that the few female scientists at King's College were treated differently than their male colleagues. That problem about the separate lunchrooms, for example, prevented women from meeting associates on an informal basis. "The lunching arrangements at King's virtually insured that, for women staff, encounters with their male counterparts were formal and unprofitable. And that such arrangements existed at all said a good deal, implicitly, about the status assigned to women, not one that could be described as equal," wrote Anne Sayre in the book *Rosalind Franklin and DNA*.

Franklin and Wilkins had a decided antipathy for each other, and the lack of a collegial relationship had significant implications for their work. "In this type of problem where the path is not straightforward, you really have to have a series of ideas one after the other," Crick later said. "If you get one of them wrong, you'll get stuck in a wrong idea. The advantage of a collaborator is that he helps you get out of those ideas."

A case could be made that Rosalind Franklin got "stuck in a wrong idea." There are two forms of DNA — the A form and the B form. Franklin had learned a great deal of information about the A form, but at one point in her work she began to study the B form and took a sharp X-ray crystallography photograph of it. "Instead of immediately dropping the work she had done on the A form and concentrating on the B form, she went plodding along with the A form, which was much more difficult to interpret," said Crick. Franklin did not think that she was "stuck in a wrong idea" or that she was "plodding along." She approached science in a methodical way. Notes written by her in November 1951 indicate that she had interpreted the clear photograph of the B form as being a helix with the phosphate groups on the outside. But for several reasons, both scientific and personal, Franklin decided to fully study the A form before turning her attention to the B form. She wasn't in a hurry; she wasn't in a "race" to find the secret of life.

Watson and Crick were first-rate collaborators. "They had almost ideally complementary gifts, and added to them exactly the compatibility that Rosalind and Wilkins lacked," wrote Anne Sayre. "Not the least significant of these gifts was Watson's knack for keeping Crick's mind fixed on the problem at hand. . . . As it has been unkindly said by one who watched the process, 'Jim nagged Francis, and it helped.' "

When Franklin firmly closed the door on Watson and Wilkins, a new bond was created between the two men.

"My encounter with Rosy opened up Maurice to a degree that I had not seen before," Watson wrote in *The Double Helix*. "Now that I need no longer merely imagine the emotional hell he had faced during the past two years, he could treat me almost as a fellow collaborator rather than as a distant acquaintance with whom close confidences inevitably led to painful misunderstandings." Wilkins confided that he had been "duplicating" some of Franklin's work and showed Watson a photo of the B structure of DNA. The photograph had been taken by Franklin. It was, strictly speaking, her property, and no one had a right to it without her permission. Years later, in a 1970 interview with Sayre, Wilkins said, "Perhaps I should have asked Rosalind's permission, and I didn't. Things were very difficult. Some people have said that I was entirely wrong to do this without her permission, without consulting her, at least, and perhaps I was. . . . If there had been anything like a normal situation here, I'd have asked her permission, naturally, though if there had been anything like a normal situation the whole matter of permission wouldn't have come up."

The entire matter might have remained a chance encounter, of no interest to anyone except the participants. But the picture, as Crick said, "gave the game away." It took Jim Watson only a few seconds to realize the significance of the X-ray photograph. "The instant I saw the picture," he wrote, "my mouth fell open and my pulse began to race."

From that moment Watson became totally preoccupied with DNA. That evening during dinner with Wilkins and during the train ride back to Cambridge from King's College in London, Watson twirled the data in his

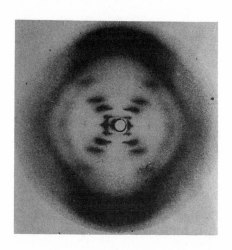

X-ray photograph of DNA in the B form, taken by Rosalind Franklin late in 1952. (From James D. Watson, The Double Helix [New York: Atheneum, 1968]; courtesy of Cold Spring Harbor Laboratory Archives)

mind. It was now clear to him that the structure was a helix because that shape seemed the best fit with the X-ray data. But did the helix consist of two strands or three? On the train he used a corner of a newspaper to jot down the data he remembered from the X-ray photograph and opted for a double-stranded helix. The next morning he rushed to the lab—even though it was Saturday—and obtained official permission from the head of the laboratory, Sir Lawrence Bragg, to embark on an all-out effort to determine the DNA code. With renewed vigor, he and Crick began a frenzy of activity. They were determined to learn the DNA structure. Over the next several days the two scientists twisted and turned parts of the model, trying to learn the structure that fit the data. It was not an easy task, and from time to time as they pursued one blind alley after another, Watson sought entertainment and refreshment, playing tennis, having dinner at Crick's apartment, and going to the movies.

Watson's love of films, developed during his childhood, had always been an important leisure activity.
Now he found that even during a movie his thoughts
wandered to DNA; he was totally dedicated to finding
the answer. Crick, too, was devoting all his efforts to the
project. Finally an idea occurred to Watson: DNA was a
double helix with identical nitrogen base sequences on
both strands so that A paired with A; T with T; G with
G; and C with C. Delighted with his new insight, he
built a model with this configuration. Watson couldn't
sleep that night thinking of the beauty of the DNA
model he had constructed. "For over two hours I happily
lay awake with pairs of adenine residues whirling in front
of my closed eyes," he wrote.

His joy was short-lived. The next morning he shared
his idea with his colleagues; the model did not withstand
scrutiny. Another scientist working in the laboratory,
Dr. Jerry Donohue, shattered the idea of like bases pairing with each other. The crux of his argument centered
on the fact that he thought the structure of the bases was
somewhat different from what had been published in a
reference book used by Watson. The two structures differed in regard to the location of the hydrogen atoms.

This was valuable new information. Watson and Crick
intensified their research. Too impatient to wait for the
machine shop to finish fashioning the models of the nitrogen-containing bases, Watson spent several hours cut-
ting out cardboard models that matched the description
given by Donohue. That accomplished, he went to dinner and the movies.

Early the next morning, he arrived at the laboratory
and began working with the models, manipulating them

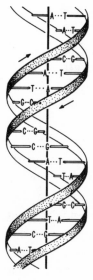

Schematic illustration of the double helix. The two sugar-phosphate backbones twist about on the outside with the flat hydrogen-bonded base pairs forming the core. Seen this way, the structure resembles a spiral staircase with the base pairs forming the steps. (From James D. Watson, The Double Helix [New York: Atheneum, 1968]; courtesy of Cold Spring Harbor Laboratory Archives)

this way and that. There must be a way for them to fit together, he thought. Suddenly the solution darted through his mind and came to rest as he slid A together with T and C with G. They fit so nicely, so beautifully. The "structure was too pretty not to be true," Watson later wrote. When Crick arrived a bit later, he agreed that the model was correct. Watson and Crick stood back and admired the structure with awe. Could it be possible? Had they indeed found the secret of life?

It was a momentous moment. After savoring it privately for a while, the two collaborators went to lunch at the Eagle Pub. "Francis winged into the Eagle to tell everyone within hearing distance that we had found the secret of life," wrote Watson. He winced a bit as the news spread. Suppose the model didn't hold up?

Their model was correct. And although Watson and Crick knew their discovery of the DNA double helix was important, even they could not foresee how many significant findings would flow from it. The DNA structure is elegant, its simplicity astonishing for a molecule that provides the chemical information of life itself. DNA carries genetic information from cell to cell and from parent to child. It is a marvelous mechanism for ensuring that a pattern for building a living organism is perpetuated from parent to offspring.

DNA, which together with protein makes up chromosomes, consists of two strands wound about each other in the form of a double helix. It is built like a twisted ladder. The sides or uprights of the ladder are made of sugar and phosphate groups. The attention-grabbing part of the molecule is the paired nitrogen-containing bases. The shapes of these bases guarantee that A always pairs exclusively with T, and C with G. This chemical partnership explains how a cell copies itself, one of the most important concepts in biology.

In order for cells to copy themselves or to form sperm or eggs (reproductive cells), chromosomes must replicate. Replication begins when the double helix "unzips." The nitrogen-containing bases, which are held together by weak hydrogen bonds, separate, creating two single strands. Each freed strand seeks new nucleotides (with A always paired with T and C with G). So a strand that consists of a section with ATCGGC, for example, must pair with TAGCCG. This partnership of complementary strands seems extraordinarily simplistic, but its simplicity guarantees that information is transmitted correctly from one cell to another and from parent to offspring.

The arrangement of the bases on DNA provides the blueprint that programs cells to make proteins, the chemicals that determine all our physical characteristics.

The sequence of the paired bases in DNA determines the kinds of proteins that are made by cells. People with blue eyes, for example, produce a different type of protein — and have a different sequence of DNA base pairs — than do people with hazel eyes. Since each human being has a unique DNA pattern, or "fingerprint," analysis of DNA can be helpful in solving crimes and in identification of individuals such as missing children.

After Watson and Crick checked to be certain their model was correct — they didn't want to be embarrassed by a public mistake — they wrote a manuscript describing their discovery. Watson's sister was asked to type the

Francis Crick and Jim Watson having morning coffee in the Cavendish, just after publication of the manuscript on the double helix. (From James D. Watson, The Double Helix [New York: Atheneum, 1968] courtesy of Cold Spring Harbor Laboratory Archives)

copy. "I remember being plopped down in front of an old-fashioned typewriter in Jim and Francis's lab," said Betty Watson. "As I began typing, we said, 'Here's to the Nobel Prize.' "

Shortly after Betty typed the manuscript, she and Jim flew to Paris for a holiday before she sailed to the United States on her way to Japan to marry Robert Myers, a young man she had met at college. For a wedding present, Jim bought his sister a beautiful umbrella at Hermès, a fashionable Parisian shop.

The article announcing the discovery of DNA appeared in the April 25, 1953, issue of *Nature*, a British science journal. J. D. Watson was listed as the first author, F. H. C. Crick as the second. How was it decided whose name

Crick's former home on Portugal Place in Cambridge. After the discovery of DNA, he named his house "The Golden Helix" and placed a single brass helix on the front. (*Photograph by and courtesy of Janet Unwin*)

should appear first? "I felt Jim really had made the key contribution by discovering the base pair," said Crick, adding that in a later paper the flip of a coin decided the order of the authors' names.

Watson and Crick began the *Nature* article with a highly reserved statement, writing, "We wish to suggest a structure for the salt of deoxyribose nucleic acid (D.N.A.). This structure has novel features which are of considerable biological interest." Watson's daydreams about announcing their discovery to the world had become a reality. We can imagine the pride he felt in writing his parents about the finding, and their happiness upon learning the news from their son, who had just celebrated his twenty-fifth birthday.

5

Balderdash and Competition

The discovery of the structure of DNA triggered a scientific revolution; it even helped to create a new discipline, the science of molecular biology. And it gave researchers insight into the study of life at a chemical level. Within a few years after the discovery of the double helix, scientists learned the mechanism by which genes direct the manufacture of proteins. "I don't think we reckoned it would go so quickly," said Francis Crick, who played a major role in many of these discoveries. "We foresaw developments, but they went rather faster than we thought." During the 1970s another discovery—of recombinant DNA techniques—surprised the scientific community. Recombinant DNA techniques allow scientists to splice small pieces of DNA from one organism to another, producing hybrid organisms. Using these techniques scientists equip bacteria with "new"

genes, enabling the altered organisms to produce sub-
stances such as insulin and antibiotics. Another appli-
cation of recombinant DNA techniques alters plant
genes, creating, for example, tomato plants that produce
fruit with improved flavor and texture. Researchers are
also exploring the use of recombinant DNA techniques
for treating inherited diseases. "We had no idea something like that would happen in our lifetimes," Crick
said. "If we were asked to guess, we would have said
sometime in the next century."

The Watson-Crick double helix is probably the most
famous of all molecular structures. Although Crick wrote
that "it is the molecule that has the glamour, not the
scientists," both he and Watson became scientific celeb-
rities. High school biology students all over the world
learn about DNA.
The names Watson
and Crick are as
firmly placed in
textbooks as those
of Mendel and Dar-
win.

*DNA is probably the
most famous molecular
structure. This model
of it is at Epcot Center
at Disney World in
Florida.* (Photograph by
and courtesy of Margaret
Hanan)

From:
M.R.C., *Laboratory of Molecular Biology*, *Hills Road, Cambridge.*

Dr. F. H. C. Crick thanks you for your letter but regrets that
he is unable to accept your kind invitation to:

send an autograph	read your manuscript
provide a photograph	deliver a lecture
cure your disease	attend a conference
be interviewed	act as chairman
talk on the radio	become an editor
appear on TV	contribute an article
speak after dinner	write a book
give a testimonial	accept an honorary degree
help you in your project	

*Besieged by requests, Crick devised this "all-purpose" card. He
says, "I usually softened the impact by writing a few words on
the back."* (Courtesy of Francis Crick)

What does one do for an encore after such a historic
finding? In his search for a scientific home, Watson
crossed the Atlantic a couple of times, working in the
United States and then in England before settling in Boston. On one flight to New York, he had the airplane almost to himself because most airline passengers were flying in the opposite direction to attend the coronation of
Queen Elizabeth II. Watson was en route to Cold Spring
Harbor Laboratory to make a public presentation of the
structure of DNA. In 1953 he accepted a position as se-

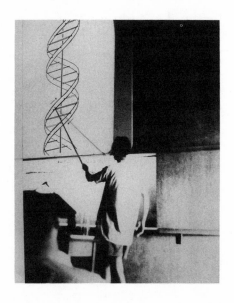

At the Cold Spring Harbor Laboratory Symposium on Quantitative Biology, 1953, Watson, dressed in shorts, explains the structure of DNA to other scientists.
(Courtesy of Cold Spring Harbor Laboratory Archives)

nior research fellow in biology at the California Institute of Technology, where Linus Pauling worked. Cal Tech was not a good fit for Watson, who later described his stay there as a time of exile. After only a year, he returned to the Cavendish Laboratory. While he was there, Dr. Neville Mott became head of the laboratory. One day Crick offered to introduce Mott to Jim Watson. "Watson?" asked a perplexed Mott. "Watson? I thought your name was Watson-Crick."

In 1956 Jim Watson joined the Harvard University faculty as assistant professor of biology. He explained his move with a one-liner designed to elicit a laugh: "I had gone on to Harvard from Pasadena because, unlike Cal Tech, it had Radcliffe girls."

Jim Watson's mother died in the spring of 1957. After her death, his dad moved to Cambridge, Massachusetts, to be closer to his son. Jim lived in a historic house, built in 1850, at 10 Appian Way; his father lived fifty feet away in a small house at 10½ Appian Way. According to an article in *The New York Times*, the younger Watson lived with "sparse furnishings, a scanty wardrobe ('enough to get by'), and a few paperbacks. . . . In contrast, the walls are covered with splendid paintings." His interest in art began, Jim said, when he "had to put something on the walls." The first artworks he owned were a drawing of a bird, which he bought at a market stall in Cambridge, England, and a Picasso print bought in Paris for $10.

Watson's arrival, plus the arrival of other scientists interested in studying DNA, marked the beginning of molecular biology at Harvard as a new way to study biology. Before the development of molecular biology, the discipline had been dominated by what some scientists called "hunters and trappers," people interested in studying the entire organism rather than cellular workings.

Jim Watson in July 1960. (*Courtesy of Cold Spring Harbor Laboratory Archives*)

"Molecular biology," said Dr. Paul Doty, who founded the Harvard biochemistry department in 1967 and became its first chair, "is the search for the ways in which interactions of molecules, usually large ones, give rise to all the species in the biological world." The two factions of biology were often at odds with each other, and in one instance Watson was nearly denied tenure in favor of a classical biologist. Although the problem was resolved and Watson received tenure, there were some rocky points in his relationship with the university administration.

Watson is sometimes described as eccentric. Tall and lanky, he has penetrating blue eyes that occasionally

A group of molecular biologists formed the informal "RNA Tie Club" to "solve the riddle of RNA structure, and to understand the way it builds proteins." The members were presented with black ties embroidered with a green-and-yellow double helix, worn here about 1955 or 1956 by Watson.
(Courtesy of
Cold Spring Harbor
Laboratory Archives)

wander off when he pauses in conversation, deep in thought. When he was a young man, his shyness was fairly apparent, and he covered it with his unusual sense of humor. He also enjoyed playing practical jokes. While at Cal Tech, he fabricated a letter to Francis Crick from Linus Pauling, inviting Crick to be an honorary visiting professor at a special symposium. He included in the letter the comment that Crick, who loved to talk, was encouraged to talk as much as he wished during the meeting. As the joke played out, even Pauling thought for a while that he might have written the letter. "The letter caused me no end of trouble," said Pauling, "because on reading it I was convinced I had written it." Eventually a grammatical error, a split infinitive, caught Pauling's attention, and he realized the letter was intended as a joke. Another of Watson's pranks involved inviting 200 people to a party he had arranged—without letting the host in on the plan. The summer had been dull, there weren't enough parties, so he decided a party would be a lively event. He invited guests to the seaside home of Dr. Albert Szent-Györgyi, a father figure in biochemistry who had won a Nobel Prize in 1937. The guests had been advised to bring food, and Szent-Györgyi accepted the prank in the jovial spirit that Watson had anticipated.

As a professor, Watson worked diligently to prepare lectures, but his students had to listen carefully to catch important information. Watson's speech pattern is unusual; he often talks softly, swallowing the ends of his sentences. Students at Harvard complained that he talked to his shirt pocket or, worse, to his shoes—but that what he said was worth hearing. "He couldn't lecture," said one of the professors. "He would stand at the board and mumble to the board." One newspaper account called him "a bumbling Jimmy Stewart." In a series of articles that appeared in the *New Yorker* and later formed part of his book *The Eighth Day of Creation,* Horace Freeland Judson wrote his impressions after attending a few sessions of a class that Watson taught at Harvard. Judson described him as a slightly bewildered professor whose glasses slipped to the end of his nose as he wrote on the board. He was, said Judson, dressed in a rumpled green suit and had "ice-blue, protuberant, even slightly wild eyes, and lips that retreat in a twitchy preoccupied smile." Watson began the first class with a statement advising students that he expected them to work hard or "find themselves with an embarrassing grade." He went on to say: "I try to distinguish those who care from those who don't. One way to tell is from the term papers. One can read term papers—but only the first five with any interest or enthusiasm. By the time you reach number twenty, you're asleep. Awful. But one thing that always does come through—even if you're asleep—in reading these papers is whether somebody is actually trying to be novel or to *think,* that's the *one* thing."

Students sitting in the back of the lecture hall could hear only segments of his sentences and called out for him to speak louder. "Yes, I'll try," he said clearly. "I know I mumble. The only way I don't mumble is if people in the back will be rude. And I don't mind. Call 'Louder' and I'll speak louder. For at least five minutes."

Despite this portrait of a "slightly bewildered professor," Jim Watson has had a major impact on many students. Dr. Nancy Hopkins was one. As a junior at Radcliffe during the early 1960s, Hopkins enrolled in an

introductory biology course at Harvard. Watson was the
second speaker in a series of invited lecturers. Hearing
him lecture electrified her and changed her life; she went
on to a career in molecular biology and is now professor
of biology at Massachusetts Institute of Technology. "He
was mesmerizing, the only experience like that I ever had
in my life. It was a revelation," she said. "He was such a
kid, really. Exciting, eccentric, young, youthful. Excited, I guess is the word. He was able to convey that this
was a revolution of major, major proportions." Did he
mumble? Yes, but Hopkins recalls the trait as a plus; it
encouraged her to sit in the first row so she wouldn't miss
a word. "You felt as though you were having a personal
conversation with him," she said. "I felt at home with
him the minute I saw him. He was a person who made
you feel [stimulated, or] on edge."

Nancy Hopkins later asked Watson if she could work
in his laboratory. He said yes. "I don't know why," Hopkins said. She enjoyed working in the lab, observing science and scientists firsthand. The large lab was con-
nected to Watson's office by a door. Sometimes he would
"fly out" to make a comment. At teatime everybody
gathered in a large central area for discussions about science and the new frontiers they were studying. It was also
the "grilling" room, a place where the young scientists
prepared for regularly scheduled seminars. "I remember
thinking this is what science is," said Hopkins, "but, of
course, there is no other Jim Watson. Nobody is as smart
as Jim Watson; he has this incredible insight." She and
Jim enjoyed having dinner together; now and then his
father joined them. She grew especially fond of the elder
Watson. "I loved his father. I would sometimes go and

see him alone," she said, adding that he was very calm, an old-fashioned person with steady, solid values, who loved baseball. "They were so different, yet they got on so well."

In addition to dining out, Jim sought relaxation at private parties. A made-for-television documentary, *The Scientist*, shows a glimpse of guests climbing the stairs to Watson's apartment in Cambridge, Massachusetts. Everyone seems to be enjoying themselves, dancing to the Beatles' recording of "All the Lonely People." Jim's expressive face is animated as he mingles with the group, offering champagne to guests and dancing with a young woman.

Although Jim Watson had no patience with those he considered to be fools, and his frank remarks might reduce a student to tears, many scientists who worked in his laboratory revered him. He did everything within his power to support bright individuals he believed to be involved in worthwhile research. He helped them secure grants or obtain equipment, and took a personal interest in each of them. He encouraged them to publish their results, and he always saw that they were credited for their work, unlike the common practice of many professors who tagged their own names on student papers before submitting them for publication. "I almost never put my name on their papers or made them think they worked for me," said Watson.

The groundwork for the new discipline of molecular biology was being forged at Harvard and at a few other prestigious laboratories. The first issues of the *Journal of Molecular Biology* were just beginning to circulate. It was such a new journal, such a new field, that sometimes

Jim Watson (left rear), Walter Gilbert (front center), and a group of laboratory workers cluster around a rhinoceros at Harvard University in the early 1960s. (*Courtesy of Cold Spring Harbor Laboratory Archives*)

Watson would check with the scientists in his laboratory to see if any of the experiments were yielding results worthy of being written up for the journal. At times the editors had to scramble to get articles to fill an issue.

Jim Watson's intelligence and personality attracted some of the best minds in biology to work in his laboratory. "He is so invigorated by his own curiosity that he makes science fun," said Dr. Paul Doty. "I think he had a sense of style that made him focus on the essentials of a problem and solve it in an elegant way." One of the scientists he recruited, Dr. Walter Gilbert, even gave up his chosen field of physics (in which he had earned a doctorate degree) to earn a second doctorate in biochemistry. Together the two men headed the committee on higher degrees in biochemistry. Eventually the Harvard department of molecular biology was founded under the leadership of Doty. It became one of the top departments of its kind in the world; pivotal pieces of information revealing how genes direct the manufacture of protein came out of their laboratory.

Dr. Joan Steitz was Watson's first female graduate student. She had hoped to work in the laboratory of another scientist, but during an interview for the position, she was asked, "What are you going to do when you get married?" The piercing question disturbed her; she burst into tears as soon as she left the office. This unfortunate occurrence actually had a silver lining since it led Steitz to work in Jim Watson's laboratory—ironically, her second choice. "It was a very exciting time to be there with all the labs involved in trying to figure out protein synthesis," she recalled. "When Jim would come back from a trip, people would cluster around him in the hall, and he would tell us what he had learned."

Steitz remembers a "very active seminar ordeal" during which students presented reports of their work. "Jim might be sitting in the back corner reading the newspaper, but he would be paying attention and would stop students after the first two sentences and say, 'OK. I don't understand a thing you're saying. Go back to the beginning and explain it properly.' " No one was coddled, and good manners fell by the wayside. Sharp, clear thinking was the reward. "Tell what you are going to say, then say it," Watson urged students. "And then tell again what you said."

Was it unnerving to be subjected to such a test? "Sure it was, but it was a lot of fun as well," explained Steitz. "They were a very exciting group of people who were bright and very interested in what they were doing—things at the forefront of science. How could it not have been exciting?" Doty said the atmosphere at the seminars was a "plus" toward stimulating good thinking and good research. "Jim Watson did introduce a quality of unobscured criticism which is still a hallmark of our department—the ability to say that something was balderdash. He was a useful critic and never suppressed any critical view of what was said by anybody. It keeps everybody sort of on the mark. There wasn't any vindictiveness about it; people learned to live with it quite happily. There was no nastiness, just an attempt to be honest." Dr. Mario Capecchi, professor in the department of human genetics at the University of Utah School of Medicine, said that Watson "doesn't hold back. He doesn't care very much about tact. If you understand it, you enjoy it. It's a breath of fresh air."

Capecchi experienced Jim Watson's unique brand of "fresh air" when he delivered an important talk on research describing how protein synthesis is terminated. He had prepared the presentation carefully and gave his report before a high-powered audience composed of top scientists from the Harvard faculty in the chemistry, biology, and biochemistry departments. Capecchi thought the talk flowed smoothly and later asked Watson what he thought, fully expecting to be complimented. Instead, Watson told him in graphic language that he thought it was one of the worst talks anybody had ever given. Why?

Capecchi, he said, had not provided enough background to explain to the group the framework on which the work rested. With the proper explanation, Watson pointed out, the significance of his accomplishment would have been better recognized. "It was very hard at the time," said Capecchi. "But it also sticks with you. After that, you try not to make the same mistake twice."

Competition, Watson says, is crucial to scientific success. A ploy he has used to advantage is projecting to his protégés the image of aggressive scientists in other laboratories pursuing the same research problem that his group is tackling. "He staged it in such a way that we felt we were competing with them," remembered Capecchi, who has found the tactic useful in his own laboratory at the University of Utah School of Medicine. "He would picture them as adversaries. In later life you found out we were quite good friends with these people." But the thrill of the race produced a stimulating environment. It pulled the group together in an "us against them" spirit that united the laboratory rather than pitting individuals in the group against each other.

Watson shared his knowledge with a broader audience by writing *Molecular Biology of the Gene*, a textbook that quickly became a classic, setting a new style and standard. It has been revised four times to keep pace with many ongoing discoveries. Watson wrote that when the first edition was published in 1965, "there were few practicing molecular biologists and not too many facts to learn." The fourth edition was published in two volumes. Watson then lamented that "DNA can no longer be portrayed with the grandeur it deserves in a handy volume that would be pleasant to carry across campus."

6

A Best-Seller

*T*he *Double Helix* sprung onto the American scene in February 1968, seizing headlines everywhere. In a front-page article *The New York Times* billed it as "a book that couldn't go to Harvard," reporting in the story that the Harvard Corporation had ruled that its Press could not publish the book; it was published instead by a noted New York publisher, Atheneum.

Francis Crick was one of the people who strongly objected to publication of the book. He wrote a six-page letter to the president of Harvard, angrily denouncing *The Double Helix* as an invasion of privacy. Copies of the letter were mailed to many people. Maurice Wilkins also protested the publication, saying it was "not a very accurate or balanced account of events."

Publication of *The Double Helix* caused a brouhaha of major proportions. It was the first book of its kind, a gossipy insider's look at the world of science. Watson had written his own personal account of the behind-the-scenes story of the discovery of the structure of DNA. He told tales about his colleagues, their struggles with each other, and the everyday life of scientists. He didn't spare himself in the account. The public was fascinated by this new genre, and the book skyrocketed on the best-seller list, remaining there for eighteen weeks. *The Double Helix* was published in full in the *Atlantic Monthly* magazine and was translated into at least seventeen languages. In a "critical edition," the original text fills only about half the book; the rest of its 298 pages are devoted to a sampling of reviews about it. *The Double Helix* changed the way people think about science. It became a classic of its kind and is read in many science and history courses. Whatever the critical view, James Watson demonstrated great success at popularizing science.

The book had its beginnings in a lecture he gave in 1962 in New York. "It provided much laughter and I knew I had to put it in print," he said. "Initially, I daydreamed that the *New Yorker* might print it under the rubric 'Annals of Crime,' since there were those who thought Francis and I had no right to think about other people's data and had in fact stolen the double helix from Maurice Wilkins and Rosalind Franklin."

Watson worked earnestly on the manuscript in 1965. "After I had a chapter tightly finished, I would give it to one or two good Radcliffe friends who were bright as well as good looking. If they would laugh, I would feel good and go on happily to the next chapter," he said. Watson was infatuated with the first line of the book: "I had never seen Francis in a modest mood." That line written, he knew he was onto something. He knew that the book would be likely to cause controversy. "No one else had written a book exactly like that," he said. Watson wanted to tell a good story in a humorous way, and he wanted to be candid. The book is sprinkled with what one reviewer called "humorously ferocious remarks." In some respects his characters were caricatures of real people. He lampooned himself with the same pen he used on others.

Watson was influenced by several authors, including C. P. Snow, F. Scott Fitzgerald, Graham Greene, and Kingsley Amis, who wrote *Lucky Jim,* a book that caused Watson to "laugh uncontrollably." Truman Capote's *In Cold Blood,* which melded fact with fiction, also influenced him. By early 1966 Watson had completed the manuscript and began showing it to other friends. The first version, said Nancy Hopkins, was "much more shocking." Some people were outraged that he was telling the story so frankly; some had a perception of the course of events that differed from his view.

The book caused such a sensation that reviewers— mostly scientists—could scarcely restrain themselves. As Dr. Gunther Stent wrote in a "review of the reviews," the articles revealed as much about the "sociology of science and the moral psychology of contemporary scientists as did the book itself."

Once during an interview, Watson gave his own "review": "I tried to write it with the same youthful arrogance I had had at the time. For some people, that came across as flippant or nasty or bright or something. I knew there would be as many people who would disagree with it as had found me impossible when I was that age. But those were the sort of attitudes I had then. I was not a lovable character. I was not going around telling people what good work they were doing! I was saying, 'You bore me!' "

"Vivid," "exciting," "tactless," "truly remarkable," "fascinating," "painful," "shallow," "shrill," and "breezy" were some of the adjectives critics used to describe the book. In a review that appeared in *Life* magazine, Philip Morrison said, "This crisp, small book is lively, wholly brash, full of sharp and sudden opinion, often at the edge of scandal." Farther along he wrote, "The book has the air of a racy novel of one more young man seeking room at the top. Censored movies, smoked salmon, French girls, tailored blazers set the stage on which ambition, deft intrigue and momentary cruelty play their roles. The story should kill the myth that great science must be cold, impersonal or detached. These young scientists covet, lust, err, hunger, play and talk about it all loud, well and long."

In an admiring assessment, Dr. Jacob Bronowski wrote that "it remains just what James Watson perceived and conceived in the beginning, a classical fable about the charmed seventh sons, the antiheroes of folklore who stumble from one comic mishap to the next until inevitably they fall into the funniest adventure of all: they guess the magic riddle correctly. Though the traditional parts of Rosalind Franklin as the witch and Linus Pauling as the rival suitor (for example) have been toned down, they are still unmistakably what they were, mythological postures rather than characters."

A hostile review by Dr. Robert L. Sinsheimer opened with the thought that "this is a saddening book, for it reminds us of that which we would rather forget—that in *Homo sapiens* brilliance need not be coupled with compassion, nor ambition with concern." His review closed with the worry that teenagers reading it would come away with the wrong idea about how science is done. "But what will be the view of the scientific endeavor to be gained by the high school student who will surely read this?" asked Sinsheimer. He or she will learn "that it is a clawing climb up a slippery slope, impeded by the authority of fools, to be made with cadged data and a resolute avoidance of profound learning, with malice toward most and with charity for none. Is this really true? Not in my experience. Rather, it is a caricature and will do far more harm than we can soon undo with sincere words about the humane and esthetic qualities of science."

In an article in the *Chicago Sun Times* another commentator stated that "James Watson was consumed with ambition for public praise and approbation, for the highest honor that a doting company of his peers could give. Surely he knows that the legitimacy of such honors depends upon the myths on which they are built. The Nobel Prize has acquired virtue by being awarded to virtuous men by virtuous men. Its total value is in its image. Yet, having craved and acquired it, Watson devalues it, debasing the currency of his own life."

Time has softened Francis Crick's view of *The Double Helix*. "My original reaction was that I didn't think anybody would read it," he said in an interview with this writer. "You can see how wrong I was. . . . Having reread it and having tried to write popular books myself, I think he did it rather skillfully. A lot of people said it read like a detective story and they couldn't put it down. There's a lot more science in it than you might have thought. I complained originally that it simplified the science, but I now know that's what you have to do."

While he was writing *The Double Helix,* Watson was

aware that the women's liberation movement was beginning to raise the level of understanding about unfair treatment of women. "Jim was the first person who alerted me to the women's liberation movement," said Nancy Hopkins. "I had never heard anyone talk about it. He was saying this about the time he was writing *The Double Helix.*" Yet he frankly told that many years earlier he and other men had treated Rosalind Franklin insensitively. To underscore his candor, Watson initially titled his manuscript *Honest Jim.* However unflattering his portrait of Franklin, without it, her contributions to science might well have remained an obscure historical footnote. By creating an archetype of a woman scientist unfairly discriminated against by male colleagues, Watson inadvertently ensured Rosalind Franklin's fame.

In an epilogue to the book, Watson wrote about Franklin, saying that his "initial impressions of her, both scientific and personal . . . were often wrong." Then he praised her work highly, saying that he and Crick "both came to appreciate greatly her personal honesty and generosity, realizing years too late the struggles that the intelligent woman faces to be accepted by a scientific world which often regards women as mere diversions from serious thinking."

Franklin's exacting X-ray crystallography work provided crucial data that helped Watson and Crick determine the structure of DNA. She was an exceedingly careful scientist, interested solely in learning what the material would reveal. Although she wasn't racing for the answer, she was close, very close to making the discovery herself. No one knows how much longer it would have taken her to discern the correct structure or even if she

Francis Harry Compton Crick in 1990.   (Photograph by Marc
Lieberman; courtesy of Francis Crick and the Salk Institute)

would have determined it. One can only guess. But such
an informed guess as that of Francis Crick is valuable.
"Perhaps three weeks," he said. "Three months is like-
lier. I'd say certainly in three months, but of course that's
a guess." When Franklin learned that the structure of
DNA had been determined, she accepted the fact with
style and grace.

Rosalind Franklin died ten years before publication of
The Double Helix. Before her death, she became friendly
with the Cricks and spent some time convalescing at
their home. "I can't say I knew Rosalind well personally,
because she was very reticent," said Crick. "She wasn't
the sort of person who would blurt everything out about

her personal life. But on the other hand she did become a friend." Crick thought Franklin was a "very good and careful experimentalist but I don't think she was quite so good on the theoretical side. . . . I don't think she realized when she took on the problem how important biologically it was. It was just another problem to be solved, and she was very interested when the solution came out. But she didn't seem to bear any sort of grudge."

It is not known how Rosalind Franklin would have reacted to the unflattering "Rosy portrait." Anne Sayre, a friend of Rosalind's, defended her against Watson's portrayal. In *Rosalind Franklin and DNA* Sayre carefully describes Franklin and her work, attempting to correct impressions that a reader might glean from *The Double Helix*. She rails against the "Rosy portrait," saying Watson "has carelessly robbed Rosalind of her personality." Sayre leaves no doubt that she is angry. "Nor is it likely that anyone, however insensitive, would quite dare to create such a picture of a living person as the one Watson created in his character of 'Rosy,' for living people have means of defending themselves which are denied to the dead."

By 1963 only eleven women were Nobel laureates, including Marie Curie, who received the award twice. Why wasn't Rosalind Franklin's name added to the list? Why wasn't she included in the stately procession of winners proudly accepting the elite award? The rules of the Nobel Foundation forbid presenting the award posthumously. And Franklin died of cancer in April 1958, four years before the Nobel Prize for the discovery of DNA was awarded. She was thirty-seven years old. Had she lived, it is a moot point whether or not she would have been awarded a Nobel since it can be shared by only three people, even though more may deserve it.

In an 1984 interview, a journalist asked Watson if Franklin deserved the Nobel Prize. "Yes," he answered. "The answer would be yes. She did the key experimental work. She did beautiful science. Equally important, after her DNA period, she went ahead and did really outstanding work on tobacco mosaic virus, its crystal structure and the location of the viral nucleic acid. I think it was apparent to everyone that she was a first-rate scientist. She did very pretty work." Today, Rosalind Franklin's contributions to science are noted in a blue plaque on the house at 22 Donovan Court in Drayton Gardens, Fulham, England, where she lived while doing the DNA work.

7

Hoping for an Angel

Jim Watson had an eye for women. He hired pretty Radcliffe coeds to work in his Harvard laboratory during the summer, to assist either with technical experiments or with editorial duties. The young women all looked fairly similar with long, straight hair and "mod" clothing, which was the current fashion. According to Mario Capecchi, who worked in the lab as a graduate student, the young women were not highly trained. "It wasn't clear that having them there was a step forward with respect to science," Capecchi said. "I think Jim hired them to liven up the place."

In the fall of 1966 a Radcliffe student, Elizabeth Lewis, came to work as a part-time secretary in the lab. A sophomore majoring in physical science, Liz was lithe, green-eyed, and had a special presence. She was the daughter of a Providence, Rhode Island, physician. Her intelli-

gence, lively conversational skills, and beauty caught Jim
Watson's attention almost immediately. He and Liz were
married on March 28, 1968, in La Jolla, California,
where Jim was attending a scientific conference. The
marriage surprised even his Harvard friends, who had
grown accustomed to thinking of Jim as a permanent
bachelor and had not realized that he and Liz had fallen
in love. They arranged their wedding spontaneously, and
the only people attending were Dr. and Mrs. Jacob Bronowski and a few other people they had invited for dinner.
Dr. Bronowski's secretary made the arrangements for the
church ceremony. Jim sent a postcard to Nancy Hopkins
announcing their marriage. Its cryptic message read,

*Jim and Liz Watson soon after their marriage in
1968.   (Courtesy of Cold Spring Harbor Laboratory Archives)*

"Now you'll have to give a real party. Jim and Liz." To other friends he wrote, "She's nineteen. She's beautiful and she's mine." It took his colleagues a while to understand that the postcards were wedding announcements.

The Watsons spent a brief honeymoon in Mexico and then went to Cold Spring Harbor Laboratory, where Jim had recently accepted a part-time position as director. The year 1968 was an important one: *The Double Helix* had been published less than two months before Jim's marriage, and he celebrated his fortieth birthday shortly thereafter. Liz found her husband youthful and forward thinking. His slim stature and boyish smile made him look younger than he was. The press was intrigued by the couple, and a cluster of articles appeared in papers and magazines about the changes in Watson's career and personal life. Liz and Jim look happy and very much in love in pictures that show Jim with his arm about Liz, smiling and solicitous of her as she fielded probing questions from curious reporters. In one photo, which appeared on a magazine cover, Liz is wearing an above-the-knee sixties-style shift and seems almost to be walking on air as she and Jim stride down a brick-lined path. In *The Scientist*, they walk hand-in-hand at Cold Spring Harbor, running downhill at one point, walking by the shore, close together, seemingly unaware of the camera marking their movements.

Jim Watson had decided to split his time between Harvard and Cold Spring Harbor Laboratory, spending summers and about a third of his winter working hours at the Long Island facility, which offered him broad new scientific and administrative challenges. His idiosyncrasies blocked him from gaining top posts at academic institutions. "He has a very funny manner; it's sort of a little bit gauche, at least superficially," Crick said. "He has a slight impediment in his speech; he gulps his words a bit and he's very uneven. . . . You hear him give a talk— sometimes it's an excellent talk and sometimes it's terrible. Those are none of the things you expect from a smooth person running something." Watson has a public persona that sets him apart. A former colleague described young James Watson as "socially inept, intellectually scattered, a weird character . . . a recipe for disaster." Yet, he could also be charming. He was ambitious, but it was unlikely that bureaucratic institutions such as Harvard or Rockefeller University would grant him a high-profile, high-power job as president. His ties to Cold Spring Harbor, on the other hand, were deep and went back twenty years. He had first gone there, as a graduate student, to attend a summer symposium. The summer symposia provided some of the best meetings, a time when eminent scientists from all over the world gathered to share their latest findings. A roster of summer courses offered researchers training in the latest scientific findings. It was one of the few places in the world where scientists could learn from experts in the field. "It was sort of your summer home," Watson explained. "In the forties and fifties it was a place where the DNA revolution began to dominate biology. So we came here."

Watson had grown very attached to Cold Spring Harbor; he was fond of its informal atmosphere and liked even the Spartan housing quarters. The cell-like rooms seemed to fit the "summer camp" style. There was no air-conditioning to relieve the sweltering temperatures, and mosquitoes bred in the bordering harbor, but he loved

SAMMIS HALL

A HISTORY OF MAN AND SCIENCE AT COLD SPRING HARBOR

DAVENPORT HOUSE

PAGE LABORATORY

DELBRÜCK LABORATORY

JONES LABORATORY   HOOPER HOUSE   WILLIAMS HOUSE

UPLANDS FARM LABORATORY

McCLINTOCK LABORATORY

CARNEGIE LIBRARY

Sketches of some of the historical buildings on the grounds of Cold Spring Harbor Laboratory.   (Illustrations by Marsha Andreola Briggs; courtesy of Cold Spring Harbor Laboratory Archives)

the place. The hot, humid weather and the rural charm encouraged informal, comfortable dress, which he preferred. He liked to wear sneakers without shoelaces, a style unusual at the time, and once, when he had a blister, he arrived at a party wearing laceless sneakers and only one sock. Watson certainly escalated the concept of unconventional dress.

Cold Spring Harbor Laboratory has a long, hallowed history of science, dating back to the nineteenth century when the Brooklyn Institute of Arts and Sciences established there the Biological Laboratory, a summer field station for biological research and education. Courses were offered in several areas of biology, and the "summer camp for scientists" became a place where teachers received firsthand experience to augment their college courses. In 1904 the Carnegie Institution founded the Station for Experimental Evolution, and in 1924 scientists and prominent Long Islanders formed the Long Island Biological Association to handle administrative responsibilities for the Biological Laboratory.

Scientists have long gravitated toward Cold Spring Harbor, finding it a congenial place to share ideas and

Jim Watson and Alfred Hershey fishing at Cold Spring Harbor in 1961. Hershey later wrote, "Jim Watson rescued the laboratory when its demise seemed likely. That was all the more remarkable because the breadth of Jim's genius could not have been anticipated at the time." (Courtesy of Cold Spring Harbor Laboratory Archives)

progress. Many significant discoveries have been made at the laboratory. In the early 1900s George H. Shull carried out landmark studies that led to the development of hybrid corn. In the 1940s, when interest in the gene began to develop, Dr. Max Delbrück and Dr. Salvador Luria shared their knowledge about bacteriophages during summer sessions. Their work laid the foundation for the research done by Dr. Alfred Hershey in 1952, which conclusively proved that DNA, not protein, was the genetic material. Hershey, Delbrück, and Luria won Nobel Prizes for their work, as did another Cold Spring Harbor scientist, Dr. Barbara McClintock, who proved that genes can "jump," or move about, on chromosomes.

Although Cold Spring Harbor Laboratory had an illustrious history, it fell into sharp decline in the early 1960s when the Carnegie Institution withdrew its support. Dr. John Cairns, who had served as director just before Watson, had modestly improved the financial standing of the laboratory, but it was being run on a shoestring. Over the years, maintenance of the buildings, many of which dated back to the 1800s or early 1900s, had been neglected. "The buildings were falling into the harbor," said Harriet "Jill" Hershey, who met her husband while working in the laboratory at Cold Spring Harbor. Watson approached the situation with offbeat élan. "I'm looking for someone who would like to give $5 million to cancer and restoring old buildings," he told a reporter. To another reporter he said, "I just love the place. I think there is a real opportunity there now, and I can influence biology more by being there than by being somewhere else, such as Harvard. I want something new to do." Since the job at Cold Spring Harbor was an unpaid position, he continued to work at Harvard, holding weekly seminars and teaching two days a week.

During his first summer as director, Watson spent time clearing out old, useless pamphlets and journals at the library. He had a keen eye for keeping what might be of historical value, but some of the accumulated material was junk to be discarded. "I don't like messes," he said of his penchant for orderliness. "He took a very active interest in how books should be arranged in the library," remembers Susan Cooper, who began her career at Cold Spring Harbor as librarian and is now director of public affairs and libraries. Watson proposed the idea of shelving some books by color. "Color was not something that I had expected to be told," said Cooper, adding that Watson had spoken about the harmony of placing the wine color of symposium volumes so that they would be seen against the blue of the harbor. Her library training had included information about grouping books by subject or in specialty collections, but color was a novel approach.

Focus on such details is characteristic of James Watson. The historic buildings, the appeal of the harbor, and the draw of first-rate science proved endlessly interesting to him. He longed to begin restoring the dilapidated buildings, but the laboratory barely had funds for the science projects.

On weekends and during the summers of 1968 and 1969, the Watsons made their home in an apartment in Hooper House on the laboratory grounds. They planned to move into Osterhout Cottage, a small house built about 1800. The attic bedrooms were cramped and miserable in summer heat waves, so they decided to renovate

Jim and Liz Watson entertain at a party for scientists attending a 1982 symposium at Cold Spring Harbor Laboratory.
(Photograph by Joan James; courtesy of Cold Spring Harbor Laboratory Archives)

and enlarge the house. In the midst of drawing up plans, the architects said it was not sensible to use the original structure, and proposed instead to build a new house for the same price as the renovations. The Watsons were delighted with their new air-conditioned home (also called Osterhout Cottage), which took advantage of the wondrous views of the harbor. Aware of the precarious state of the laboratory's finances, and enriched by royalties from *The Double Helix*, Watson donated the funds for the construction project, although the home became the property of the laboratory.

Watson's taking over the reins of the Cold Spring Harbor Laboratory involved tackling complicated administrative responsibilities. Among the early decisions he had to make were determining the research focus and finding a staff to carry it out. "Much of staffing is dominated by intellectual objectives," he explained, adding that choosing the people to fit into the general scheme enhances intellectual collaboration. His education at the University of Chicago had emphasized "ends," stressing that you should "know where you want to go before you decide how to get there."

One of Watson's strengths is his ability to target a problem that is ripe for solving. In August 1968, a newspaper article headlined "James (Double Helix) Watson— A Watsonian Era?" quoted a student as saying, "His greatest talent is his uncanny instinct for the important problem, the thing that leads to big-time results. He seems to pick it out of an item in a professional magazine or pluck it out of thin air." Watson encouraged his students to tackle difficult problems that might lead to important results. "I believe in the *now*," he is quoted as saying, "to hell with being discovered when you're dead."

Watson chose the study of cancer to be the core of Cold Spring Harbor Laboratory research. He selected this focus from among many other potential fields of study. His intuition led him to concentrate on a group of viruses, some of which experimentally can cause cancer. He selected viruses that have few genes and could be easily studied. Among them were SV40, which causes cancer in monkeys, and human viruses called adenoviruses, which produce symptoms similar to the common cold.

He located and hired the best tumor virus researchers he could find and sought grants to support the laboratory. In 1969 one of the newly hired researchers, Dr. Joseph Sambrook, was awarded a $1.6 million grant. The laboratory began to bloom.

One of Watson's most challenging jobs as laboratory director was fund-raising. Federal grants were important to the support of the lab, but he hoped to find an "angel" benefactor. In his first director's report, he wrote, "There also remains the fact that the Lab badly needs a real benefactor, but with much love it will probably survive without one. Of course, I dream an angel will appear soon and make me free of any serious worries for at least a month."

In an interview with a Long Island reporter, Watson repeated his wish. John Davenport, a retired pharmaceutical company executive, read the article and fulfilled Watson's hopes by donating sufficient funds to cover half the costs of building an addition to one of the laboratory's buildings.

8

A Village of Science

*J*im and Liz Watson continued to divide their time between Harvard and Cold Spring Harbor. Their first child, Rufus, was born in 1970, and two years later another son, Duncan, completed the family.

Liz Watson, who had earned her undergraduate degree at Radcliffe, had become increasingly interested in architectural preservation. She audited an art history course at Harvard and began to think of pursuing an advanced degree. She earned a certificate in the practical training course of the New York School of Interior Design and then earned a master's degree in historic preservation at the Columbia University Graduate School of Architecture and Planning.

Liz was also busy as a hostess at Cold Spring Harbor. As a young bride, she took an active interest in cooking, studying cookbooks in the evening hours when Jim returned to the lab after dinner. One of the first recipes that she polished to perfection was *boeuf Bourguignon.* And she developed a raft of quiche recipes, handy for

*The Watson family relaxes on the grounds of Airslie. This
photograph was sent as a Christmas card in the late
1970s.   (Courtesy of Cold Spring Harbor Laboratory Archives)*

entertaining. The Watsons welcomed scientists, members of the Board of Directors, and neighbors to their
home. The luncheon and dinner parties were a meld of
the professional and personal interests that dominated
their lives. "You had someone to lunch and hoped they
liked us and would help us get the lab going again," Watson said of the lunches he and Liz hosted. One of the
lunches, it turned out, would have a major impact on the
laboratory.

   In July 1972, while the Watsons were vacationing in
California, they learned that Charles Robertson, a phi-

lanthropist whose deceased wife had been heir to the fortune generated by the A & P grocery store chain, had expressed interest in visiting the laboratory. The Watsons set a date to entertain Robertson. At the lunch that Liz prepared at Osterhout Cottage, Robertson discussed the framework for giving his estate in nearby Lloyd Harbor to the laboratory. He added a gift of $8 million to establish the Robertson Research Fund. Income from the endowment could be used to provide supplementary support to research grants.

Now the laboratory could move into higher gear, buy needed equipment, and repair its buildings. The Robertson Fund also helped solve a difficult problem with regard to a marina located on the shore of the harbor opposite the laboratory. Plans to expand the marina were halted when the laboratory purchased the site, thus preserving one of Long Island's last remaining salt marshes. An association rents the existing marina and pays an annual fee for that privilege.

The Robertson Fund also helped ease a personal dilemma for the Watsons. Dividing their time between Cambridge, Massachusetts, and Long Island, New York, was becoming increasingly difficult as their sons approached school age. Since only Harvard paid Watson a salary, he and Liz had been juggling their lives between the two places. The Robertson Fund made it possible for Watson to begin drawing a salary from Cold Spring Harbor Laboratory and for the family to live there full-time.

Saying farewell to Harvard was like closing a chapter in Jim Watson's life. It was there that he had matured and taken on the role of directing science. He bade an emotional good-bye to his colleagues at Harvard. "It's the most emotional I've ever seen him," said Dr. Mark Ptashne, professor of biochemistry and molecular biology. "There's a whole side to Jim that's very historically oriented, very conservative and institutionally oriented. I think Harvard was for him the ideal thing; he had such tremendous impact on building our department. I remember seeing him practically in tears. His leaving was a tribute to his honesty, because it wasn't as though we said 'Jim, you have to go.' Jim said, 'You can't have someone in the department simultaneously building another place.' He engineered his own departure and was profoundly distressed by leaving here."

When the Watsons moved to Cold Spring Harbor full-time, they moved from Osterhout Cottage to Airslie, the large federal-style farmhouse that had been built in 1806 for Major William Jones, a relative of the first patron of the laboratory. Airslie served not only as their home but as the focal point of the entertaining that is an integral part of the director's responsibilities. Before moving in, they hired Charles Moore Associates, now the Centerbrook Architects and Planners, to design plans to renovate the house. Charles Moore, a renowned architect and teacher, approached the renovation with skill and flair, introducing impressive architectural elements and lighting and a spectacular entrance highlighted by a staircase reaching to the third floor. The grounds of Airslie are dotted with large old trees, among them cork, magnolia, and chestnut. The front lawn slopes to the harbor and is often the site of parties for laboratory staff members and visitors.

Beauty and design are important to Jim Watson. He involved himself in every detail of decision making about the renovation. "As is probably evident from the subject of his Nobel Prize, he has a good sense of structure and is interested in how things go together and how things relate to each other spatially," said William Grover, an architect who is a partner in Centerbrook Architects and Planners. "He also understands, partly as a result of his having been in England, how the quality of a research institution reflects the intellectual atmosphere in that place." No item was too trivial for him. Grover wrote that the architects "spent hours divining the exact curve of a driveway that would satisfy Jim Watson's sense of balance and symmetry." To help Watson visualize the form of the driveway, the architect placed sticks at strategic locations and enlisted the aid of several people to act as physical guideposts in defining the path. Years later, Watson spoke to a reporter about his interest in visual perfection. "Architecture dominates us," he said. "I like how things look. It's that simple. I find it relaxing. A beautiful girl, a beautiful tree, a beautiful painting. I like beautiful sentences. . . . One of my unrealistic ambitions is to think that four hundred years down the line you'd think of Cambridge [England], Harvard and Cold Spring Harbor because of their visual impact."

As monies became available and as scientific needs arose, Watson made certain that renovations were done to his meticulous standards. He looked at buildings in New York and Boston to help sharpen his ideas and told the architects to avoid designing buildings that looked like banks. He made sure that public areas were kept simple without ostentatious displays of marble and fountains: The Watsons were careful to preserve the feel of the place. The laboratory has the sense of a New England fishing village. In the early years when the laboratory budget was slim, wood was used to construct the buildings. Increased funding later allowed use of more durable materials such as masonry, brick, stone, and slate roofs. To avoid a harsh look, slick lab benches are offset by wooden bases. Newer buildings blend in with the older structures, and the laboratory, though greatly expanded, retains a rare sense of peace and charm.

As full-time director, James Watson revved up the pace of fund-raising and recruited and nurtured the best scientific minds he could find. One such scientist is Dr. Phillip Sharp, now head of the department of biology at the Massachusetts Institute of Technology. At Cold Spring Harbor, Sharp's lab was next to Watson's office in the James Laboratory. "As Jim walked back and forth to his office, particularly at night when he was not involved in other things, he'd stop from time to time and ask what was going on," Sharp said. "Jim would seldom offer any detailed advice as to whether you should do this or that or how it would work, but he showed interest, and that made you think about things in new and interesting ways. As a piece of research came near completion, he would make sure to come around and say, 'Well, are you writing it up now?' " When a paper was completed, Watson would read it and then perhaps suggest that Sharp give it to Alfred Hershey, who was a good editor and had a style for saying the most with the least number of words. Watson encouraged the scientists in many ways and acted as their mentor. "Much of science is transmitted in terms of conversations about what's going on, what's interesting and what's new," said Sharp, explaining the informal network that exists among scientists.

"Jim made sure that one's work was recognized in those conversations."

Watson's decisions concerning which type of research problems to pursue began to realize significant gains. He had anticipated the national assault on cancer, officially launched in 1971 by President Richard Nixon as the War on Cancer. The laboratory benefited from additional federal funds earmarked for cancer research. Important discoveries started to mount up in the 1970s regarding restriction enzymes, which are useful tools in recombinant DNA procedures. Several key findings were made at Cold Spring Harbor Laboratory, including the discovery by Dr. Richard Roberts of seventeen of these new enzymes.

Restriction enzymes are called "molecular scissors" because of their ability to chemically cut DNA at specific locations, allowing scientists to insert foreign genes. The concept of combining pieces of DNA in novel ways caused great consternation among scientists, who worried that genetically altered organisms might get out of control and cause havoc. Top scientists proposed a moratorium restricting certain areas of recombinant DNA research until more information could be gathered. Watson initially agreed with this position, but at a March 1975 conference at the Asilomar Conference Center on the Monterey Peninsula in California, he found himself uneasy that scientists were no longer talking about a limited ban on research but were focusing instead on how the restrictions could be expanded.

"From the start I felt most out of tune," he later wrote, explaining elsewhere that he thought "the matter was becoming hopelessly overblown." The National Institutes of Health (NIH) developed guidelines regarding some areas of research. Watson's voice was loud and clear in national debates. He wrote forceful articles explaining his position. In a 1978 editorial he said that "now . . . we are in a strange mess. . . . All because some people have spread the word that DNA, the stuff which makes up our genes, might do us all in. I find this assertion total nonsense and cannot think of any potential environmental pollutant which worries me less." In another article, "In Further Defense of DNA," he explained, "Recombinant DNA, per se, is not something first brought forth by science. It is an obligatory fact of life whose occurrence is far wider than generally perceived. Viruses, for example, have the potential to cross species barriers and to carry DNA between unrelated organisms."

In the *Washington Post* Watson wrote an article headlined "The Nobelist vs. the Film Star," in which he took Robert Redford's Environmental Defense Fund and other environmental groups to task for attempting to block recombinant DNA experimentation. "The test-tube-made genetic material now provides an incredibly powerful means to find out what human genes are like," he wrote. "And in so doing it will give us important new ways to think, say, about our immune systems, or how our blood cells are made or the nature of the genes that go out of control when cancer arises." Elsewhere in the article he wrote, "Compared to almost any other object which starts with the letter *D*, DNA is very safe indeed. Far better to worry about daggers, or dynamite, or dogs or dieldrin [an insecticide] or dioxin or drunken drivers, than to draw up Rube Goldberg schemes on how our laboratory-made DNA will lead to the extinction of the human race.

"The strains of viruses and cells we work with in the laboratory generally are not pathogenic for man, and all we know about infectious diseases makes it unlikely that the addition of a little foreign DNA will create any danger for those who work with recombinant DNA-bearing bacteria."

Watson thought it important to take a national stand, in part to support the ongoing work at Cold Spring Harbor Laboratory. He was concerned that regulations would curtail research aimed at isolating cancer-causing genes and learning how they worked. In the late 1970s, his view prevailed, and the NIH guidelines were changed to allow recombinant DNA research to flourish. A few years later, a Cold Spring Harbor research group found the *ras* oncogene. A group at another institution made the same discovery simultaneously. Damaged forms of oncogenes can change normal human cells into cancer cells. Watson's decision to focus on cancer research years earlier led to this major discovery and to others as well.

Laboratory scientists, many of them young people in their twenties and thirties, work long hours, often late into the night and on weekends. Watson thinks the competition among them is key to stimulating good science. The Cold Spring Harbor Laboratory researchers have no teaching or administrative responsibilities, so they can concentrate completely on research. In some respects the laboratory is a training ground. Many scientists come there only for a few years and then go on to more permanent appointments at universities. Some scientists who hold senior positions are given "rolling five" appointments, Watson's version of contracts that run for five years. For the most part the researchers are young

Scientists visiting for summer meetings in the late 1970s attend a
wine-and-cheese party on the lawn in front of Airslie.   (Courtesy
of Cold Spring Harbor Laboratory Archives)

and eager to work furiously at the leading edge of science.

Intellectually, Cold Spring Harbor Laboratory has long been considered *the* place to exchange ideas and share firsthand in the latest discoveries. Every summer scientists flock to the north shore of Long Island to attend the popular seminars. Under Watson's guidance, the number of summer seminars increased steadily. In 1974 a record of over 300 people attended the symposium on tumor viruses.

As research thrived, the lovely Cold Spring Harbor grounds were continually refurbished under the Watsons'

guidance. The Jones Laboratory, built in 1893, was ren-
ovated in 1975. Two years later the Williams House was
rebuilt as an apartment complex. The growing laboratory
needed a water treatment plant; Watson was unhappy
with the engineering decree that mandated its location
near the water. He didn't want the utilitarian structure

*The model of the
adenovirus atop the
gazebo built over the
wastewater treatment
plant.* (Photographs by
Harvey Weber; courtesy of
Cold Spring Harbor
Laboratory Archives)

to mar the view, so the architects designed a Victorian-style structure topped by a gazebo that overlooks the harbor. Perched on the roof of the gazebo is a sculptural figure holding aloft a model of an adenovirus, a type of virus that affects humans. "Jim and I looked through his book *Molecular Biology of the Gene*," said William Grover, in explaining how the adenovirus model was selected. "I suggested a strand of DNA, but he said, 'That's old hat, it should be an adenovirus.'" Grover made the copper model and presented it as a gift. When it was put in place, Watson had the workman readjust it six degrees, a slight amount to anyone else's eye but significant to his. The stylish treatment plant is often the site for wedding photos; participants are unaware of the plant's function.

Another building, located at the entrance to the laboratory grounds, clearly had seen better days. The paint on Davenport House was flaking; its porch and roof were sagging. Built in 1884, the half-timbered Victorian structure with its dramatic embellishments had substantial promise, however, and the Watsons resolved to restore it to its original grandeur. They located a carpenter with the expertise to reproduce the intricate woodwork. Determining the exact colors of the original paint became a major challenge. Liz Watson worked closely with an expert; they used a scalpel to probe through layers of old paint to extract chips of the base color. Altogether fifty-four samples were scrutinzed microscopically. The original colors were revealed to be deep-hued vibrant Victorian shades of pumpkin, golden yellows, hearty greens, and maroon. "The hardest part," Mrs. Watson said later, "was selling my husband on the idea of the original paint colors." Today, the colorful Davenport House stands as a welcoming sentinel, a vivid grande dame inviting visitors to turn off the main road, Route 25A, and enter the Village of Science.

Davenport House, which has been splendidly restored. (Photograph by the author)

9

Mapping Genes

"Isn't there another way around this?" Jeff Goldblum asked laughingly as he was about to get a close-cropped haircut. The actor had recently grown his hair long for playing the lead role in the movie *The Fly*, and he liked the look. Now he needed a crew cut to play Jim Watson in a made-for-television movie. Filmed by the British Broadcasting Corporation and the Arts and Entertainment Network, the movie had different titles depending upon where it was shown. In England it was called *Life Story*; in the United States it was billed as *Race for the Double Helix*, a punchier title thought to have greater appeal to the American public.

In addition to Jeff Goldblum, the cast included Tim Pigott-Smith as Francis Crick, Juliet Stevenson as Rosalind Franklin, and Alan Howard as Maurice Wilkins. William Nicholson, the writer, and an assistant spent several months researching material for the script and interviewing people.

The movie opens with a scene in Naples with Watson

and his sister, Betty, in conversation. Within a few minutes, the importance of DNA and Watson's interest in it
are set forth. Goldblum portrays a somewhat nervous,
hyper Jim Watson whose gaze moves rapidly, perhaps
mirroring the abrupt shifts of his mind jumping from one
point to another. Goldblum plays up the image of Watson's interest in young women, and he chews gum. It was
not Watson's habit to chew gum, but Goldblum has his
jaws in constant motion, perhaps to help him catch Watson's speech pattern of gulping his words at the ends of
sentences.

The story moves quickly from Naples to Paris (where
it introduces Rosalind Franklin) and then to London
where Watson and Crick meet. "We all rather looked
like ourselves," said Betty Watson Myers. For a long time
Jim Watson could not bring himself to watch the movie.
When he finally saw it, he thought it "was done very
well," adding that watching a movie about oneself is a
strange experience. He was bothered by some things that
weren't exactly right: Certain actors were too old for
their parts; he didn't quite look like Jeff Goldblum; and
he was no longer so thin.

The film brought renewed attention to the DNA double helix story and to Watson, a founding father of molecular biology. "Sometimes I feel I'm a living historical
figure," he said, explaining how strange it is to be approached for his autograph.

James Watson has received honorary degrees from several universities, including Notre Dame, Harvard, and
Rockefeller. In 1988, he was honored by Rutgers University, the state university of New Jersey. "Research scien-

Watson autographs a book for a student at the Margaret Cameron Spain Auditorium, University of Alabama at Birmingham, November 15, 1988. (Courtesy of Cold Spring Harbor Laboratory Archives)

tist, author and administrator, yours was the rare joy of seeing what mankind had not theretofore seen," said Edward J. Bloustein, president, as he bestowed the doctor of science degree. "Participant in one of the major scientific events of this or any century, recipient of the 1962 Nobel Prize in Physiology or Medicine, your vision of the DNA molecule as a double helix had an elegance which transformed the sciences of biochemistry and genetics and is now central to the increasingly significant science of molecular biology. Your book, *The Double Helix,* admirably conveys the excitement of your discovery, and

President Gerald Ford congratulates Watson after presenting him with the Medal of Freedom award, January 10, 1977. (Courtesy of Cold Spring Harbor Laboratory Archives)

reinforces the con-cept of science as the preeminent hu-man adventure."

One of Watson's most prestigious awards is the Medal of Freedom, the nation's highest civilian award. He learned of the honor when he received a call from the White House in early January 1977. It "was a great way to begin the new year," he said. The award was presented by President Gerald Ford in a ceremony that honored twenty-one other Americans, including Lady Bird Johnson, Vice President Nelson Rockefeller, Joe DiMaggio, Irving Berlin, and Norman Rockwell.

Given James Watson's prominence, it was not a surprise that in October 1988 he was tapped to head the National Center for Human Genome Research. It was thought that a man of Watson's stature would be influential in getting Congress to fund the genome research

A smiling Jim Watson on his sixtieth birthday in 1988. (Photograph by Sue Zehl; courtesy of Cold Spring Harbor Laboratory Archives)

project. A flurry of magazine and newspaper articles trumpeted his arrival. Called biology's "moonshot," the research project is a $3 billion, fifteen-year effort. The project was controversial when first suggested because many scientists feared that money for such a giant effort would drain dollars away from other research projects. Watson's appointment helped quell the criticism.

The human genome is all the DNA in twenty-three chromosomes—between 50,000 and 100,000 genes. It contains the instructions for making a human being. The goal of the project is to map the location of each of these genes and determine the sequence of nitrogen-containing bases in our DNA.

The DNA blueprint tells a great deal about a person, including susceptibility to genetic diseases. By studying your DNA, someone someday may be able to tell if you might become diabetic later in life or be likely to suffer a heart attack. "Many of the disorders that dominate our world, such as heart disease, cancer, arthritis, alcoholism and mental illness, may be caused by genetic abnormalities," Watson has pointed out. "As we analyze the information hidden within the chemical composition of every gene in the human body, the role of medicine will shift from treatment to prevention." It is expected that the genome research project will eventually lead to a cure for many diseases. It may one day be possible, for example, to treat diabetes by replacing one or more of the defective genes. "That's the dream," said Watson.

As director of both the genome research project and of Cold Spring Harbor Laboratory itself, Watson often groaned at being overcommitted. His workdays were longer than ever, and the pace more hectic. He split his time between Long Island and Washington, D.C., commuting two days a week to the nation's capital and keeping in touch by telephone and fax the rest of the time. "It's taking increasingly more and more of my time," Watson said of the project. "I thought I could escape if I was down there only two days a week, but I wasn't aware of the power of the fax to absolutely pin one down at a moment's notice."

Watson's sharp vision and intelligence shaped the project in important ways. Dr. Elke Jordan, deputy director of the National Center for Human Genome Research, says of Watson, "It's fascinating how he always looks to the future. He cares much less about what's going on today. That's a very useful perspective, because in a bureaucracy you tend to be absorbed by what's happening today. Dr. Watson is able to turn his vision to the future." In designing the project, Watson dealt with ethical considerations and also established large research groups, rather than relying on individual investigators working alone. These two elements, Jordan says, were "absolutely crucial to making the project work right."

The first element addressed the social implications of the research. What might happen, Watson and other experts asked, if genetic information were to fall into the "wrong hands"? Insurance companies or employers, for instance, who had information about a person's DNA might use it to discriminate against that individual. But such information would be especially valuable in patient-doctor relationships. It would offer guidelines for altering one's life-style to prevent a disease from developing and would promote early treatment. It is expected that eventually many diseases will be treated with gene therapy; Watson foresaw the need to consider how this new knowledge might impact on society.

Watson knew it was important "to worry about the ethics from the start." Initially he proposed spending 3 percent of the $3 million budget to support the ethics of DNA studies; eventually that figure was increased to 5 percent. Watson appointed Dr. Nancy Wexler to head the ethics committee. She is a prominent genetics researcher who has identified herself as being at risk for a serious genetic condition called Huntington's disease.

The second major element Watson addressed was shaping the research so that a few relatively large groups of scientists work together on projects. "Creation of these large groups has turned out to be just the right thing, because they are much more efficient at doing big jobs," said Elke Jordan.

To promote the genome research project, Watson gave

many interviews and presented scores of talks. His unique intensity, combined with a sense of humor, won friends for the project. And he worked to get other countries to join in gene research. Some of the data from the project will be commercially useful, and Watson thinks that the cost of obtaining it should be shared by countries that will benefit from it. He was disturbed that Japan might not contribute its fair share to the work. When his concern became public, he was accused of Japan bashing. "I've found you never get anywhere in the world by being a wimp," Watson told a reporter for the journal *Science*, characteristically standing firm for his beliefs.

A major issue arose in the early 1990s following the appointment of Dr. Bernadine Healy to head the National Institutes of Health (NIH). Technology had advanced to where it was possible to identify fragments of genes rapidly. These fragments are chunks of DNA with no known function, but they are helpful in determining the location of a gene. Healy thought that the NIH should patent these fragments. "I would like to emphasize that NIH's goal in patenting any discovery, including a gene, is not to make money," Healy said, "but rather to promote and encourage the rapid development and commercialization of products to improve human health, and to do so in a socially responsible way." The idea of patenting gene fragments of unknown function struck Watson as "sheer lunacy." He and other scientists were outraged at the idea and felt it would hinder research. A story in the *Wall Street Journal* explained that "Dr. Watson isn't against patenting genes per se. Indeed, patents are the financial incentive that drives a great deal of research. Dr. Watson worries, however, that by tying up enormous stretches of genes at a time—through the wholesale patenting of their fragments—the NIH will discourage others from devoting the resources needed to discover the full nature of these particular elements of the genome."

Watson considered resigning from his post as head of the genome research project. The job was so time consuming; indeed it required a full-time director. In April 1992, other concerns arose over conflict-of-interest questions regarding some of Watson's stock holdings. He had made a full disclosure of his holdings, and the NIH legal adviser for ethics suggested the matter could be put to rest if Bernadine Healy would sign a waiver. She, however, was not willing to do this. Watson believed that Healy wanted him to resign, and so on April 10, he issued a letter of resignation. In an interview with reporters from the *Washington Post,* he said, "I have a fine reputation, and they are trying to soil it when I've worked very hard for three and a half years on behalf of the country. I would say this is the lowest moment of my life—to work so hard and to be treated so badly." Having spoken forthrightly, he refused to talk further with the press about his resignation.

He returned to Cold Spring Harbor Laboratory full-time and set to work with renewed vigor. The appointment of Dr. Bruce Stillman as assistant director in 1990 had freed Watson from some day-to-day administrative responsibilities, allowing him to attend to long-range goals such as fund-raising. Today he concentrates his energies on the laboratory he loves.

A hat shields Watson from the sun's rays in a photograph taken in 1992.   (Photograph by the author)

He also has time for personal pleasures. Jim and Liz still enjoy strolling the laboratory grounds, as they have since they first came to the lab in 1968. "A thing I respect a lot about Jim and his wife, Liz," said Dr. Daniel Marshak, "is that after twenty some years of marriage, they are more in love, I think, then they've ever been." A member of the laboratory research staff, Marshak added, "When I see them walking down the road hand in hand admiring the beautiful sunset, I try to emulate that with my wife. I like the idea of solid family life and not losing sight of the fact that your spouse is a very special person and that you have to work hard at keeping those relationships going."

Liz Watson autographs a copy of Houses for Science *for Dr. Barbara McClintock in 1991.* (*Photograph by Margot Bennett; courtesy of Cold Spring Harbor Laboratory Archives*)

Over the years Liz Watson has contributed a great deal to preserving and restoring historic laboratory buildings. Her book, *Houses for Science, A Pictorial History of Cold Spring Harbor Laboratory,* is a splendid chronicle of the history of the laboratory and a guide to the architectural details of its buildings. Jim contributed to it a series of essays about genetics. He and Liz plan to build a new home on a site along the harbor with magnificent water views and a distant view of the Connecticut shore. Jim wants another building plan to provide athletic facilities and child care for the laboratory's scientists and visitors. He wrote about the need for this new building in an annual report, citing that physical activities "provide easy ways to start speaking to strangers." Watson understands that communication in science often occurs in informal settings and can be the key to effective research. He completed his report by saying "I have much work cut out for me in the near future."

10

A University of DNA

The Cold Spring Harbor Laboratory celebrated its one hundredth year in 1990. James Watson has shepherded the lab through more than one-fifth of its existence and can be proud of his work there. The laboratory was near collapse when he became its director in 1968. He rescued it and turned it into a major cancer research center. His pioneering decision to study tumor viruses led to significant discoveries, including many restriction enzymes, the *ras* oncogene, and a link between cancer-causing genes and cancer-suppressing anti-oncogenes. New research focuses on the workings of the cell cycle in an effort to learn what triggers cells to move from phase to phase during cell reproduction.

The laboratory has grown enormously under Watson's leadership. "In coming here, I never asked myself whether we could continue to do inspired science in the

past manner of Barbara McClintock and Alfred Hershey," he wrote in 1988. "Then, my thoughts focused
primarily on the Lab's survival. . . . So the fact that we
have operated at a world-class level for virtually all of the
last twenty years gives me pleasure that I never anticipated and so never initially worried about." Today the
laboratory is a world leader in molecular biology with an
operating budget of more than $33 million. More than
500 people work full-time on its staff. Important scientific meetings and courses take place on its grounds. More
than 12,000 people, including seventy-five Nobel Prize
winners, attended the fifty-five Symposia on Quantitative

*Watson speaks with a student in the Partners for the Future
program in September 1991 as her mother and an educator
listen.*   (Photograph by Margot Bennett; courtesy of Cold Spring Harbor
Laboratory Archives)

Biology, which began in 1933. The laboratory hosted
only two symposia in 1968. Twenty years later that number had jumped to twenty-five meetings. Watson has pre-
dicted that by the year 2000, the lab will have to host
some fifty meetings if it is to continue as the premier
meeting place in the world for biology. The meetings are
now held in an elegant new auditorium. *Forbes* magazine
named Cold Spring Harbor Laboratory one of the "best
addresses in American Science."

Watson advises teenagers interested in a career in the
sciences to "come into contact with people who do sci-

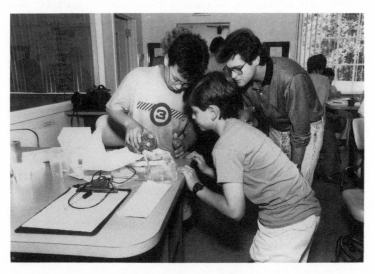

*Students carry out a DNA experiment in the Bio2000 classroom
in the summer of 1991 as David A. Micklos, director
of the DNA Learning Center, supervises.* (Photograph by Susan
Lauter; courtesy of Cold Spring Harbor Laboratory Archives)

ence, so you can see how they behave and how they think, because at some stage, you must test yourself against them. You have to be able to ask them intelligent questions and reply to their questions. If you want to become a great tennis player, you must play with better tennis players. Ambitions should be focused. If you think you don't have to go where the action is, that's a mistake." Each year, five Long Island high school seniors are accepted into a highly competitive program sponsored by the lab. Called Partners for the Future, it allows students to work with scientist mentors. During the school year these teenagers spend ten hours weekly working at the laboratory and being at the forefront of the action.

The laboratory's DNA Learning Center, located in a former school building in Cold Spring Harbor, provides elementary and high school students and their teachers an opportunity to learn firsthand about DNA. In a special classroom lab called *Bio2000*, they perform experiments using molecular biology techniques. The refurbished elementary school houses several exhibits that introduce visitors to DNA.

In the 1990s—proclaimed by President George Bush as "The Decade of the Brain"—Cold Spring Harbor Laboratory made a major leap forward with the opening of the $22.5 million Neuroscience Center. The new complex could have been a startling addition to the quiet "Village of Science." Instead it blends serenely with its surroundings, nestled into a hillside setting. It can barely be seen from across the harbor during the spring and summer months when trees are in leaf. The complex consists of two buildings that provide housing and laboratory facilities. A tower in the courtyard is reminiscent

Balloons herald the opening of the Neuroscience Center on May 3, 1991. (Photograph by Margot Bennett; courtesy of Cold Spring Harbor Laboratory Archives)

of a campanile in a European city. Its bronze bell rings the hour throughout the day. The tower camouflages chimneys and has a helical staircase that serves as a re-minder of the DNA structure and, more functionally, provides a fire escape. Golden letters—*a, t, c, g,* the ini-tials of the bases in DNA—are inscribed at the top of the tower. William Grover, the architect, likes the little in-side clues that people "in the know" understand. When his daughters, Amy and Gigi, were young, Grover told them that the *a* and *g* inscribed in the tower were their initials.

In the new Beckman Laboratory in the complex, hall-way and office floors are covered by gray carpeting flecked

The tower in the courtyard of the Neuroscience Center. Each of its four sides bears an initial of the nitrogen-containing bases in DNA.
(Photograph by Ed Campodonico; courtesy of Cold Spring Harbor Laboratory Archives)

Jim Watson in his office in the Beckman Laboratory building in 1992.   (Photograph by the author)

with maroon; white oak paneling offers a soothing contrast to stark laboratory benches. When the building
opened, Watson moved from the James Laboratory to the
second floor of the Beckman Laboratory. His office is
simply and elegantly furnished. The walls behind his
desk provide display space for a well-organized array of
paintings, photographs, and his Nobel Prize. Other photos in the office are of his sons, and of himself at work in
his Harvard office; there is a caricature of Watson and
Crick as well as a print by the Spanish painter Joan Miró.
On his desk is a picture of Liz. Another wall holds a
collection of art that Watson has gathered on his travels
around the world, including a painting called the *Couple*

This illustrated certificate of the Nobel award hangs on the wall
behind Watson's desk.   (*Photograph by Ed Campodonico; courtesy of*
Cold Spring Harbor Laboratory Archives)

in the Moon, which he bought in Calcutta, and a sculp-
ture that caught his eye in New Guinea. Of his art collection, Watson says, "I like art. You have to fill up the
walls with something." Covers on ceiling light fixtures in
the conference area of his office and throughout the
Beckman Laboratory feature DNA "fingerprint" patterns.

While the Neuroscience Center was under construction, Watson grappled with choosing the most effective
research approach for studying the functions of learning
and memory. His decision-making ability still leaves
many of his colleagues in awe. One of these colleagues,
Bruce Stillman, says that Watson often makes a radical
proposal and throws it out on the table. "A lot of people
might be taken aback by it," notes Stillman, adding that
the first reaction often provides facts that are the most
informative. When Watson feels he's wrong, he listens
to the reaction and modifies his position or even reverses
it. He sometimes comes up with what people call "off-
the-wall proposals," but many of them make good sense
when fully analyzed. "There's no formal decision-making
process here," Stillman reports. "It gets done by people
running into each other on the road. Some of the most
important conversations that we've had have been out on
Bungtown Road [the main road of the laboratory]. Jim
and I pass each other, and we get talking about things."

One of the things that Jim Watson talked about with
Stillman and other scientists was the possibility of using
the common fruit fly, *Drosophila melanogaster,* to study
learning and memory. At one time this organism seemed
promising as a genetic model for these research areas, but
it had not yielded much information. The idea intrigued

Crick and Watson take a break between meetings at a
symposium on the brain in 1990.   *(Photograph by Ed Campodonico;*
courtesy of Cold Spring Harbor Laboratory Archives)

Watson but held little interest for other scientists. He
brought it up at a special 1990 symposium on the brain.
"Every single person on the advisory board [of the Neuroscience Center] advised us not to do this," Stillman said.
Other scientists who gathered at a picnic held during the
special meeting agreed with the majority. Yet Watson
wasn't dissuaded. The more he thought about the idea,
the more sense it made. "It was partly, I think, because
Cold Spring Harbor didn't want to follow along with
what other people were doing," said Stillman. "I see this
decision to work on *Drosophila* as similar to Jim's decision
to work on DNA tumor viruses." So Jim Watson made

another courageous decision: to devote at least half of the new research effort to the study of fruit flies.

In a room on the top floor of the Beckman Laboratory, scientists use "teaching machines" to study the learning ability of these tiny organisms. The researchers expose fruit flies to two different odors. One odor is coupled with a slight electrical shock. The flies learn to associate the shock with the odor and to avoid that odor. Although more than 90 percent of the fruit flies tested are capable of learning, scientists discovered that some were mutant strains incapable of learning. These flies, nicknamed dunce, amnesiac, turnip, and rutabaga, are valuable in helping to isolate the memory gene and its protein. If Watson's decision to focus on learning in fruit flies is as

Friends of the laboratory ride in the Rotifer, *a replica of a boat used at Cold Spring Harbor in the late 1800s, during the 1990 celebration.* (Photograph by Susan Lauter; courtesy of Cold Spring Harbor Laboratory Archives)

Members of the laboratory's first biology class held in 1890 and their 1990 counterparts, who reenacted the scene for the centennial celebration. (Recent photograph by Margot Bennett; both photographs courtesy of Cold Spring Harbor Laboratory Archives)

good as his decisions have been in the past, scientists will soon comprehend at the molecular level how neurons learn and remember—and understand how humans, as well as lowly fruit flies, think.

The Neuroscience Center and the building housing the Grace Auditorium are real breaks with the past, Watson says. These buildings have raised the laboratory to a new status, making it a different kind of institution. There were few conveniences at Cold Spring Harbor Laboratory when Watson first arrived. Most of the buildings didn't even have heat. Under his directorship the laboratory has achieved near-university status. Watson is fond of calling it a "university of DNA."

Although the laboratory's centennial celebration stretched over three years, the main festivities took place on July 14, 1990, when more than 1,600 people gathered for the event. In the afternoon a small boat made its way through the harbor. "Come see the *Rotifer*," called a smiling Jim Watson to some of the visitors. His wispy hair blew in the wind while he stood on the shore watching a reenactment of a scene from a hundred years ago. Robert Gensel of the laboratory's purchasing department had studied an old picture from the archives and gathered friends of the laboratory to bring the photo to life. As the boat came close, the "actors," dressed in period costumes, doffed their hats and waved to the people on the shore. Later they assembled on the steps of the Jones building to restage a gathering of the laboratory's first biology class.

At a special ceremony, Watson was presented with several proclamations commemorating the centennial. "Your devotion to the pursuit of knowledge has led to some of the most important scientific discoveries of our time," wrote President George Bush in a letter applauding the laboratory researchers on their achievements. The Forebitter, a group of sea chantey singers, and other musicians provided music throughout the day. Guests enjoyed a large-scale barbecue on the lawn by Blackford Hall. The grocery list included 1,900 sausages, 3,000 hot dogs, 3,600 pieces of chicken, forty gallons of clam chowder, 1,300 ears of corn, 2,400 pickle spears, and 450 pounds of potato salad. Jim and Liz Watson seemed to be everywhere, chatting with guests, rushing up Bungtown Road to Airslie, where another dinner was being hosted under a tent. Afterward there was a concert on Davenport lawn and a spectacular round of fireworks.

As Jim Watson wandered the grounds that day, he felt a strong sense of kinship with the landscape and the buildings on the campus, many of which bear his stamp architecturally; the science conducted within their walls is administered by him. Watson's enlightened vision and devotion have preserved the history and beauty of Cold Spring Harbor Laboratory, while enabling it to flower as a world-class research center. The historic discovery of the structure of DNA in 1953 helped catapult science into an unprecedented era of genetic research, begun a century earlier with Mendel's concept of the gene. Unlike Mendel, who died before his work was recognized, Jim Watson continues to participate in the scientific revolution that followed the landmark discovery of the DNA double helix.

Glossary

adenine (A)—a nitrogen-containing base in DNA

adenoviruses—several viruses that cause upper respiratory tract infections similar to the common cold

bacteriophage (or phage)—a virus that attacks bacteria and multiplies in them

chromosome—a structure in a cell nucleus composed of DNA and protein that appears rodlike during cell division; the chromosomes carry the genetic material

cytosine (C)—a nitrogen-containing base in DNA

deoxyribonucleic acid—see DNA

deoxyribose—the five-carbon sugar present in DNA

DNA (deoxyribonucleic acid)—the component of chromosomes that carries genetic information

DNA "fingerprinting"—a technique that compares DNA in individuals; used in forensic medicine and to prove maternity and paternity

Drosophila melanogaster—see fruit fly

egg—a female reproductive cell

fruit fly (*Drosophila melanogaster*)—a tiny fly useful in genetics studies

genetic code—the code used by all living things to translate genetic information into protein

genetics—the study of genes and heredity

guanine (G)—a nitrogen-containing base in DNA

helix—a spiral or coil shape

human genome—all the DNA in twenty-three chromosomes; it contains the instructions for making a human being

microorganism—a living thing that is visible only under a microscope

molecular biology—the study of living cells at the biochemical and molecular level

mutation—a change in DNA that is inheritable

nitrogen-containing base—a single- or double-ringed organic compound with one or more nitrogen atoms

nucleotide—a building block of a nucleic acid (DNA and RNA); contains a sugar (deoxyribose in DNA; ribose in RNA), a phosphate group, and one of four nitrogen-containing bases

oncogene—a damaged form of a type of gene that controls some aspect of cell growth; oncogenes can change normal human cells into cancer cells

ornithology—the study of birds

phosphate group—a group of atoms consisting of one phosphorus atom bonded to four oxygen atoms

proteins—large molecules composed of amino acids

recombinant DNA—hybrid DNA produced by combining DNA from two sources

restriction enzymes—chemicals that can be used to cut DNA molecules at specific locations

ribonucleic acid—see RNA

ribose—the five-carbon sugar present in RNA

RNA (ribonucleic acid)—helps translate genetic message in DNA into protein; exists in three forms

sperm—a male reproductive cell

SV40—a virus that causes cancer in monkeys

thymine (T)—a nitrogen-containing base in DNA

tumor viruses—viruses that in a laboratory setting can change normal cells into cancer cells

virus—a particle made of DNA or RNA and protein that is on the borderline between living and nonliving; reproduces only in a living cell; one-tenth the size of a bacterium

X-ray crystallography—a technique that uses X rays to study the structure of materials that crystallize, including proteins and DNA; X-ray crystallography is still the only way to determine a molecule's structure atom by atom

For Further Reading

Crick, Francis. *What Mad Pursuit. A Personal View of Scientific Discovery.* New York: Basic Books, 1988.

Davis, Monte. "The World According to Jim." *Discover*, April 1981, 40–43.

Edson, Lee. "James (Double Helix) Watson—A Watsonian Era?" *New York Times Magazine*, August 18, 1968.

Franklin-Barbajosa, Cassandra. "The New Science of Identity." *National Geographic*, May 1992, 112–24.

Hall, Stephen S. "James Watson and the Search for Biology's 'Holy Grail.' " *Smithsonian* 20, no. 11 (February 1990): 40–49.

Jaroff, Leon. "The Gene Hunt." *Time* 133, no. 12 (March 20, 1989): 62–67.

Judson, Horace Freeland. *The Eighth Day of Creation. Makers of the Revolution in Biology.* New York: Simon and Schuster, 1979.

Limburg, Peter R. "James D. Watson." *Science Year 1990*, World Book Annual Science Supplement, 339–51.

Sayre, Anne. *Rosalind Franklin and DNA*. New York: Norton, 1975.

Watson, Elizabeth L. *Houses for Science. A Pictorial History of Cold Spring Harbor Laboratory*. Plainview, N.Y.: Cold Spring Harbor Laboratory Press, 1991.

Watson, James D. *The Double Helix. A Personal Account of the Discovery of the Structure of DNA*. Norton Critical Edition. Text, Commentary, Reviews, Original Papers, ed. Gunther S. Stent. New York: Norton, 1980.

Other References

Anderson, Christopher. "U.S. Genome Head Faces Charges of Conflict." *Nature* 356 (April 9, 1992): 463.

Andrews, Joan Kostick. "The Man Who Makes Cold Spring Harbor Tick." *The World & I*, July 1990, 322–25.

Baldwin, Joyce. "Writing a New Chapter to 'Double Helix' " (Long Island interview with James D. Watson). *New York Times*, April 9, 1989.

Barry, John M. "Cracking the Code." *The Washingtonian*, February 1991.

Beck, Kirsten. "Science That Soars." *Channels*, November 1988.

Berg, Paul, et al. "Potential Biohazards of Recombinant DNA Molecules." *Science* 185, no. 4148 (July 26, 1974): 303.

Bradbury, Will. "Genius on the Prowl." *Life*, October 30, 1970, 57–66.

Breo, Dennis. "DNA Discoverer James Watson Now Dreams of Curing Genetic Diseases." *JAMA* 262, no. 23 (December 15, 1989): 3340–43.

Brown, David, and Malcolm Gladwell. "Nobel Prize Biologist Watson Plans to Resign U.S. Position." *Washington Post*, April 9, 1992, A3.

Campbell, Neil A. "Discoverer of the Double Helix." *Bio-Science*, December 1986, 728–730.

Cooke, Robert. "Dean of DNA . . . Gene Mapmaker." *Newsday*, January 24, 1989, Discovery (Part III), 1.

Cooper, Robert C. "The Rebirth of a Legend. Chicago's New Regal Theater." *Emerge: Our Voice in Today's World*, June 1990, 68–69.

Crick, Francis. "How to Live with a Golden Helix." *The Sciences*, September 1979, 6–9.

Current Biography. "James (Dewey) Watson," 1990, 605–9. Fox, Jeffrey L. "The DNA Double Helix Turns 30." *Science:* 222, no. 4619 (October 7, 1983): 29.

Davis, Bob. "Watson Doesn't Use Gentle Persuasion to Enlist Japanese and German Support for Genome Effort." *Wall Street Journal*, June 18, 1990, A12.

"Frenetic Genetics." *Radio Times*, April 25–May 1, 1987, 82–83.

Harbor Transcript (a newsletter). Spring 1989 to summer 1992, Cold Spring Harbor Laboratory.

Healy, Bernadine. Remarks presented at Public Meeting of FCCSET Committee on Life Sciences and Health Genome Patent Working Group, May 21, 1992, Washington, DC.

Hiltzik, Lee R. "The Director, the Laboratory, and the Genome Project: An Interview with James D. Watson." *Long Island Historical Journal* 2, no. 2 (spring 1990): 163–69.

Indiana Alumni Magazine. "James D. Watson, Ph.D. '50 Becomes First Graduate to Win Nobel Prize." November 1962, 6.

"James Watson to Head NIH Human Genome Project." *Nature* 335 (September 15, 1988): 193.

Johnson, George. "Two Sides to Every Science Story," *New York Times Book Review*, April 9, 1990.

Jones, Tony. "The Unravelling of the Double Helix" (review of BBC film, *Life Story*). *New Scientist*, April 23, 1987, 55.

Lane, Earl. "Inside James Watson's World-Famous Lab." *LI. Newsday's Magazine for Long Island*, February 4, 1979, 10.

Liversidge, Anthony. "Interview. James D. Watson." *Omni*, May 1984.

McKusick, Victor A., ed. *The Human Genome.* A special issue of *Hospital Practice* 26, no. 10 (October 15, 1991).

Micklos, David. *The First Hundred Years, Cold Spring Harbor Laboratory.* Cold Spring Harbor, NY: Cold Spring Harbor Laboratory, 1988.

O'Connor, John J. " 'Double Helix,' On A&E." *New York Times*, September 14, 1987, C14.

O'Neill, Maureen. "Biologist Shares a Little 'Madness.' " *Newsday*, February 5, 1981, 21.

Reinhold, Robert. "Watson, Author of 'The Double Helix,' to Direct Laboratory on Long Island." *New York Times*, March 28, 1968.

Roberts, Leslie. "Watson May Head Genome Office." *Science* 240, no. 4854 (May 13, 1988): 878.

Robertson, Nan. "Nobel Scholar Becomes an Impresario of Pure Science." *Chicago Tribune*, January 24, 1981, Sec. 1, p. 13.

Schmeck, Jr., Harold M. "DNA Pioneer to Tackle Biggest Gene Project Ever." *New York Times*, October 4, 1988, 1.

———. "Nobel Winner to Head Gene Project." *New York Times*, September 27, 1988, 6.

————. "Reporter's Notebook: Watson Took His Place up Front." *New York Times*, April 19, 1983, 2.

Shapley, Deborah. Review of *Rosalind Franklin and DNA*, by Anne Sayre. *New York Times Book Review*, September 21, 1975, 27.

Smith, Roger. "For James D. Watson Challenge at Cold Spring Harbor." *Scientific Research*, April 29, 1968, 36–37.

Stahle, Nils K. *Alfred Nobel and the Nobel Prizes*. Stockholm: Nobel Foundation, Swedish Institute, 1989.

Stout, Hilary. "Watson, Head of U.S. Genome Project, Faces Questions over Stock Holdings." *Wall Street Journal*, April 9, 1992, B8.

Sullivan, Walter. "A Book That Couldn't Go to Harvard." *New York Times*, February 15, 1968.

————. "The Competition Can Get Personal." *New York Times*, February 18, 1968, Sec. 4, 8.

Thompson, Larry. "Gene Pioneer Will Head Mapping Project." *Washington Post*, September 27, 1988, Health, 7.

————. "The Man Behind the Double Helix," *Washington Post*, October 12, 1989.

"Twenty-one Years of the Double Helix." *Nature* 248, April 26, 1974, 721.

Unger, Michael. "The Land of DNA." *Newsday*, July 10, 1990, Discovery (Part III).

Waldholz, Michael, and Hilary Stout. "A New Debate Rages over the Patenting of Gene Discoveries." *Wall Street Journal*, April 17, 1992.

Watson, James D. "In Defense of DNA." *New Republic* 170 (June 25, 1977): 11–13.

————. Director's Report in Annual Reports, 1968–72 and 1987–91: Cold Spring Harbor Laboratory.

———. "Growing Up in the Phage Group." In *Phage and the Origins of Molecular Biology*, ed. J. Cairns, G. S. Stent, and J. D. Watson. 239–45. Plainview, N.Y.: Cold Spring Habor Laboratory Press, 1992.

———. "Lecture on Excellence" presented before the LTV Washington Seminar, Washington, D.C., 1981. In *Excellence: The Pursuit, the Commitment, the Achievement*, Corporate Affairs Department of the LTV Corporation, Dallas, Texas, 1981, 32–41.

———. "Minds That Live for Science." *New Scientist*, May 21, 1987.

———. "The Nobelist vs. the Film Star." *Washington Post*, May 14, 1978, D1–D2.

———. "Trying to Bury Asilomar" (editorial). *Clinical Research* 26 (1978): 113–17.

Watson, James D., and F. H. C. Crick. "Molecular Structure of Nucleic Acids." *Nature* 171 (April 25, 1953): 737–38.

Watson, James D., and John Tooze. *The DNA Story. A Documentary History of Gene Cloning*. San Francisco: Freeman, 1981.

Watson, James D., et al. *Molecular Biology of the Gene*. 4th ed. Menlo Park, Calif.: Benjamin/Cummings Publishing, 1987.

Watson, James D., and Norton Zinder. "Genome Project Maps Paths of Diseases and Drugs" (letter). *New York Times*, October 13, 1990, 24.

Whelan, W. J. "The Other Half of Watson." *Trends in Biochemical Sciences*, April 1978, N89.

White, Kristin. "Medical Treasure in a Moral Thicket." *Loyola Magazine* 19, no. 3 (winter 1991): 5–12.

Wiskari, Werner. "Nobel Prize Goes to 3 Biophysicists." *New York Times*, October 19, 1962.

Zinman, David. "A Biologist Probes the Virus of Unrest." *Newsday*, June 19, 1970, 4A–5A.

————. "L. I. Scientist Picked to Map Genes." *Newsday*, September 27, 1988, 6.

————. "Scientist Begins His and Lab's New Life." *Newsday*, April 6, 1968, 11.

————. "Watson Asked to Lead Genetic Project." *Newsday*, May 18, 1988, 6.

————. "What's Wrong with Cancer Research: A Nobel Laureate Speaks Out." *LI. Newsday's Magazine for Long Island*, September 23, 1973.

Index